Enhancing Professional Practice *A Framework for Teaching*

Charlotte Danielson

 Association for Supervision and Curriculum Development
Alexandria, Virginia

Association for Supervision and Curriculum Development
1703 N. Beauregard St. • Alexandria, VA 22311-1714 USA
Telephone: 1-800-933-2723 or 703-578-9600 • Fax: 703-575-5400
Web site: http://www.ascd.org • E-mail: member@ascd.org

Gene R. Carter, *Executive Director*
Michelle Terry, *Associate Executive Director, Program Development*
Nancy Modrak, *Director, Publishing*
John O'Neil, *Acquisitions Director*
Julie Houtz, *Managing Editor of Books*
Margaret Oosterman, *Associate Editor*
Gary Bloom, *Director, Editorial, Design, and Production Services*
Karen Monaco, *Senior Designer*
Tracey A. Smith, *Production Manager*
Dina Murray, *Production Coordinator*
Valerie Sprague, *Desktop Publisher*

ASCD Stock No. 196074
Member $16.95
Nonmember $19.95
November 1996 member book (pc). ASCD Premium, Comprehensive,
and Regular members periodically receive ASCD books as part of
their membership benefits. No. FY97-2.

Library of Congress Cataloging-in-Publication Data

Danielson, Charlotte.
   Enhancing professional practice : a framework for teaching /
Charlotte Danielson.
      p.   cm.
   Includes bibliographical references.
   ISBN 0-87120-269-7
   1. Teaching. 2. Classroom environment. 3. Educational planning.
I. Title.
LB1025.3.D35   1996   96-25256
371.1'02—dc20   CIP

04   03   02   01   00   12   11   10   9   8   7

ABOUT THE AUTHOR

Charlotte Danielson is a program administrator for Educational Testing Service (ETS) in Princeton, New Jersey. She has taught at all levels, from kindergarten through college; worked as a consultant on curriculum planning, performance assessment, and professional development for numerous schools and school districts in the United States and overseas; and designed materials and training programs for ASCD, ETS, and the National Board for Professional Teaching Standards.

In addition to authoring *Enhancing Professional Practice: A Framework for Teaching*, Danielson developed an ASCD Professional Inquiry Kit, *Teaching for Understanding*. Her work has encouraged assessment in the service of learning by both teachers and students.

Danielson can be reached at Educational Testing Service, Mail Stop 14-D, Rosedale Road, Princeton, NJ 08541 USA. E-mail: cdanielson@ets.org

I *came into this school year expecting, as well as fearing, a lot. A lot of everything. I guess because it's a new start so I can have a completely new experience.*

I suppose I expect the most from myself as a scholar, a friend, and a part of the community. I expect to do as well as I can in every class every day. I expect myself not to become discouraged if I don't do as well as I expected to do on a test or anything else.

I expect my fellow students to be as supportive to me and the rest of the class as I am to them. I want to always feel comfortable speaking in class.

I expect my teachers to always listen to every student as an equal and to always be fair.

These are the words of a 9th grade student describing her expectations at the beginning of a new year in a new school. We must never forget the students' voices as we, the professional educators, plan for their academic success. This book is dedicated to all students, who entrust their daily lives to their teachers.

ENHANCING PROFESSIONAL PRACTICE:
A FRAMEWORK FOR TEACHING

Foreword

I walked into the classroom, hands trembling, knees knocking. I tried to look composed and sophisticated (which can be difficult for a young, short person). The class waited expectantly. That's all I remember from my first day of teaching 25 years ago. The feeling of panic remains with me, the details forgotten. I wish I'd had some help to get through those first few weeks—from a colleague, in writing—anything to dissolve the knot in my stomach.

Some time later, in a different classroom, I introduced a lesson on creative writing by reading the beginning of a short story. The students delighted in my playing all the roles—something about watching a teacher act like an idiot, I think. I stopped reading at a critical moment in the plot and asked each student to write an ending. Their papers were fascinating, showing imagination and logic, and giving me insight into their thinking. They had clearly been engaged in learning—and I was thrilled. I wish I'd had a forum where I could have shared my experiences and received some tips on how to improve the lesson.

Enhancing Professional Practice: A Framework for Teaching offers the type of guidance I could have used to enhance my teaching. It provides a "road map" to guide novice teachers through their initial classroom experiences, a structure to help experienced professionals become more effective, and a means to focus improvement efforts.

The framework groups teachers' responsibilities into four major areas, which are clearly defined and further divided into components. Figures for the components show the specific elements that teachers need to focus on. When I was a new teacher, I could have used the elements in "managing classroom procedures" to help develop self-confidence in what I was doing. While observing my creative writing lesson, my colleague could have used the "classroom observation record" to identify and discuss the strong and weak points of the lesson and my teaching skills.

Engaging all students in learning is our primary mission as educators, and Charlotte Danielson makes this the unifying thread of the framework. All stakeholders—teachers, colleagues, parents, and the larger community—are needed to reach this goal. The structured dialogue about teaching offered here makes attainment easier, while helping us become better educators.

—FRANCES FAIRCLOTH JONES
ASCD President 1996–97

PREFACE

n 1987, Educational Testing Service (ETS) began a large-scale project to provide a framework for state and local agencies to use for making teacher licensing decisions. The resulting program is called The PRAXIS Series: Professional Assessments for Beginning Teachers®. Many states use PRAXIS I: Computer-Based Academic Skills Assessment and PRAXIS II: Subject Assessments to grant an initial teaching license. PRAXIS III: Classroom Performance Assessments is for use in assessing actual teaching skills and classroom performance.

I worked with ETS to help prepare and validate the criteria for PRAXIS III. The criteria were based on formal analyses of important tasks required of beginning teachers; reviews of research; analyses of state regulations for teacher licensing; and extensive field work that included pilot testing the criteria and assessment process (Dwyer and Villegas 1993; Dwyer 1994; Rosenfeld, Freeberg, and Bukatko 1992; Rosenfeld, Reynolds, and Bukatko 1992; Rosenfeld, Wilder, and Bukatko 1992).

My particular responsibility in the development of PRAXIS III was to design the training program for assessors. Because the PRAXIS system is used to license beginning teachers, assessors for PRAXIS III must be able to make professionally and legally defensible judgments. Indeed, throughout the pilot and field testing of both the instrument and the training program, the rates of interrater agreement were high.

As valuable as PRAXIS III is for states in the licensing of qualified teachers, I came to see its usefulness as extending far beyond that limited role. In training hundreds of assessors to use the PRAXIS III framework for assessing the teaching of novices, I witnessed the quality of the participants' conversation. It became clear that in their daily lives, educators have (or make) little opportunity to discuss good teaching. As participants watched videotapes and read scenarios of teaching during the assessor training, they had to determine how what they observed represented the application of the various criteria in different contexts. For example, they noticed that a kindergarten teacher's actions to help students extend their thinking were quite different from those employed by a chemistry teacher. And yet, both teachers might be extending their students' thinking; so both sets of action constituted examples of a particular criterion in different contexts.

As educators (particularly teachers) watched and discussed the videotapes with one another, they also engaged in side conversations or reflection about their own teaching. That is, they saw a teacher's action that they could adopt or adapt to their own setting. They heard a teacher phrase a question such that it provoked deep thinking by

students—and they might determine to try something similar. Hence, as teachers went through the training program, they interacted with the activities on several different levels. On the surface, of course, they were preparing to become certified assessors, which meant that they had to pass a proficiency test. On a deeper level, they were finding that the conversations themselves were helpful and that their own practice would be changed as a result.

Because of its impact on their own teaching, many PRAXIS III assessors reported that the experience of training was some of the most powerful professional development they had ever participated in. It gave them a structured opportunity to discuss teaching with colleagues in a concrete and research-based setting. Such opportunities are indeed rare in our schools. A participant's statement expresses the thinking of many: "By participating in the PRAXIS III training, I have focused more on my own teaching. I have become more thoughtful in my teaching and more concerned that my instructional activities fulfill my goals." I, too, was changed by the experience. I developed a profound appreciation for the power of structured conversation to enrich the professional lives of teachers.

To restrict such conversations to those who serve as PRAXIS III assessors in states that choose to use that framework for licensing beginning teachers appeared to be too narrow an application. What about teachers in every state? What about those who already have their license? What about those who supervise student teachers or mentor beginning teachers? Wouldn't all those relationships and experiences be enriched by a comprehensive framework for teaching?

This line of thinking resulted in *Enhancing Professional Practice: A Framework for Teaching*. The framework is based on the PRAXIS III criteria, augmented to apply to experienced as well as to novice teachers and used for purposes beyond the licensing of beginning teachers. It is a framework that will, I hope, enrich the professional lives of those who choose to use it.

Other work also influenced the development of the framework: documents from the standards committees of the National Board for Professional Teaching Standards (NBPTS); work at the University of Wisconsin (Newmann, Secada, and Wehlage 1995); Michael Scriven's (1994) conceptions of teacher duties; and recent research on the pedagogical implications of constructivist learning. The framework has been subjected to a further intensive review by ETS colleagues: Carol Dwyer, Ruth Hummel, and Alice Sims-Gunzenhauser. The research foundation for the framework is provided in the Appendix.

ACKNOWLEDGMENTS

In the completion of this project, I am indebted to Educational Testing Service and the opportunity afforded me there to participate in what I believe to have been educationally significant work. Of the many individuals with whom I worked, I would like to especially recognize Paul Ramsey, who recommended me for the project; Carol Anne Dwyer, who managed the project; Alice Sims-Gunzenhauser, who coordinated the development of the criteria; Ruth Hummel, who worked in all aspects of the project but especially in the coordination of field work and assessor training; and Roberta Camp, Carol Myford, and Ana Maria Villegas, who provided insights through their many research studies. In addition, I would like to thank the educators in the partner development states of Delaware and Minnesota, who generously shared their experience and expertise to improve both the system and the training program. I also owe a special thanks to colleagues all over the country (Steve Gring, Marilyn Lindquist, Phyllis Levy, John Pennoyer, Rich Swartz, Mary Diez, Georgea Langer, and

Karolyn Snyder, among others), who have reviewed earlier drafts of the manuscript and offered their suggestions for improvement. Lastly, Carol Anne Dwyer, Ruth Hummel, and Alice Sims-Gunzenhauser participated in a final round of meetings on the components themselves and the levels of performance and helped ensure their comprehensiveness and compatibility with the criteria used in PRAXIS III: Classroom Performance Assessments.

1

A FRAMEWORK FOR TEACHING

The framework for teaching described in this book identifies those aspects of a teacher's responsibilities that have been documented through empirical studies and theoretical research as promoting improved student learning. Although not the only possible framework, these responsibilities seek to define what teachers should know and be able to do in the exercise of their profession.

In this framework, the complex activity of teaching is divided into 22 components clustered into four domains of teaching responsibility: planning and preparation (Domain 1), classroom environment (Domain 2), instruction (Domain 3), and professional responsibilities (Domain 4). Each component defines a distinct aspect of a domain; two to five elements describe a specific feature of a component. For example, Domain 2, "The Classroom Environment," contains five components. Component 2a is "Creating an Environment of Respect and Rapport," which consists of two elements: "Teacher interaction with students" and "Student interaction." This component applies in some manner to all settings. But while teachers at all levels and in all subjects establish rapport with and convey respect for their students, they do so in different ways. Figure 1.1 (see pp. 3–4) summarizes the components and their elements; Chapter 6 describes them in detail.

Although the components are distinct, they are, of course, related to one another. A teacher's planning and preparation affect instruction, and all these are affected by the reflection on practice that accompanies a unit and lesson. In addition, many features of teaching, such as the appropriate use of technology or a concern for equity, do not each constitute a single component but rather apply to them all. Chapter 3 identifies those common themes that apply to many of the components.

> The components of professional practice are a comprehensive framework reflecting the many different aspects of teaching.

WHY HAVE A FRAMEWORK?

A framework for professional practice is not unique to education. Indeed, other professions—medicine, accounting, and architecture among many others—have well-established definitions of expertise and procedures to certify novice and advanced practitioners. Such procedures are the public's guarantee that the members of a profession hold themselves and their colleagues to the highest standards. Similarly, a framework of professional practice for teaching is useful not only to practicing educators but also to the larger community, because it conveys that educators, like other professionals, hold themselves to the highest standards.

A framework for professional practice can be used for a wide range of purposes, from meeting novices' needs to enhancing veterans' skills. Because teaching is complex, it is helpful to have a road map through the territory, structured around a shared understanding of teaching. Novice teachers, of necessity, are concerned with day-to-day survival; experienced teachers want to improve their effectiveness and help their colleagues do so as well; highly accomplished teachers want to move toward advanced certification and serve as a resource to less-experienced colleagues.

COMPLEXITY OF TEACHING

The complexity of teaching is well recognized; a teacher makes over 3,000 nontrivial decisions daily. It is useful to think of teaching as similar to not one but several other professions, combining the skills of business management, human relations, and theater arts:

• Business managers set goals for groups of subordinates and try to lead them toward accomplishing the goals. Such managers must allocate time and other scarce resources as they balance task and socioemotional considerations. They distribute rewards and sanctions to those in their charge. Similarly, teachers must motivate students to engage in learning; set goals and subgoals; manage time and other resources; and be accountable for the results.

• Human relations work involves understanding the dynamics of a large group of individuals, each with a complex set of needs and

Figure 1.1

Components of Professional Practice

Domain 1: Planning and Preparation

Component 1a: *Demonstrating Knowledge of Content and Pedagogy*
- Knowledge of content
- Knowledge of prerequisite relationships
- Knowledge of content-related pedagogy

Component 1b: *Demonstrating Knowledge of Students*
- Knowledge of characteristics of age group
- Knowledge of students' varied approaches to learning
- Knowledge of students' skills and knowledge
- Knowledge of students' interests and cultural heritage

Component 1c: *Selecting Instructional Goals*
- Value
- Clarity
- Suitability for diverse students
- Balance

Component 1d: *Demonstrating Knowledge of Resources*
- Resources for teaching
- Resources for students

Component 1e: *Designing Coherent Instruction*
- Learning activities
- Instructional materials and resources
- Instructional groups
- Lesson and unit structure

Component 1f: *Assessing Student Learning*
- Congruence with instructional goals
- Criteria and standards
- Use for planning

Domain 2: The Classroom Environment

Component 2a: *Creating an Environment of Respect and Rapport*
- Teacher interaction with students
- Student interaction

Component 2b: *Establishing a Culture for Learning*
- Importance of the content
- Student pride in work
- Expectations for learning and achievement

Component 2c: *Managing Classroom Procedures*
- Management of instructional groups
- Management of transitions
- Management of materials and supplies
- Performance of noninstructional duties
- Supervision of volunteers and paraprofessionals

Component 2d: *Managing Student Behavior*
- Expectations
- Monitoring of student behavior
- Response to student misbehavior

Component 2e: *Organizing Physical Space*
- Safety and arrangement of furniture
- Accessibility to learning and use of physical resources

Components of Professional Practice *(continued)*

Domain 3: Instruction

Component 3a: *Communicating Clearly and Accurately*
   Directions and procedures
   Oral and written language

Component 3b: *Using Questioning and Discussion Techniques*
   Quality of questions
   Discussion techniques
   Student participation

Component 3c: *Engaging Students in Learning*
   Representation of content
   Activities and assignments
   Grouping of students
   Instructional materials and resources
   Structure and pacing

Component 3d: *Providing Feedback to Students*
   Quality: accurate, substantive, constructive, and specific
   Timeliness

Component 3e: *Demonstrating Flexibility and Responsiveness*
   Lesson adjustment
   Response to students
   Persistence

Domain 4: Professional Responsibilities

Component 4a: *Reflecting on Teaching*
   Accuracy
   Use in future teaching

Component 4b: *Maintaining Accurate Records*
   Student completion of assignments
   Student progress in learning
   Noninstructional records

Component 4c: *Communicating with Families*
   Information about the instructional program
   Information about individual students
   Engagement of families in the instructional program

Component 4d: *Contributing to the School and District*
   Relationships with colleagues
   Service to the school
   Participation in school and district projects

Component 4e: *Growing and Developing Professionally*
   Enhancement of content knowledge and pedagogical skill
   Service to the profession

Component 4f: *Showing Professionalism*
   Service to students
   Advocacy
   Decision making

desires. A teacher must also consider the range of individual personalities and take advantage of any opportunities for motivating students. In addition, a teacher must be able to connect with diverse students and establish relationships of caring and concern.

• Theater arts include many types of professionals, such as director, stage manager, actor, set designer, and even playwright. Teachers must be the equivalent of all the theater arts components. And although a director can, for example, delegate responsibility for props and sets, a teacher must manage all materials. Moreover, teachers may have to follow a script they do not particularly like, and the "audience" is frequently not attending voluntarily.

Other metaphors come to mind. Teachers have been likened to orchestra conductors, gardeners, engineers, and artists. Indeed, depending on which aspect of the job one is considering, any of these references may be appropriate. Many metaphors include students, such as Theodore Sizer's "student as worker; teacher as coach." These metaphors remind us of the intellectual and emotional demands of teaching and the many, sometimes competing, aspects of the job.

But even more demanding than its complexity is the level of stress that teaching generates. Planning for the productive activity of 30 or more individuals (some of them present reluctantly) and successfully executing those plans, all within the context of multiple (and sometimes conflicting) demands from the school, district, community, and state, leave many teachers—particularly novices—buffeted, confused, or discouraged. The physical demands of the job are daunting, requiring enormous stamina. Most teachers leave school exhausted at the end of the day, knowing that their students will return the next day rested and ready for more. "Will I be ready?" teachers ask themselves. "Can I be ready? What will we *do* all day? How will I engage my students so that I can maintain control and they will learn something significant?"

GUIDANCE FOR PROFESSIONAL CONVERSATION

A framework for professional practice offers the profession a means of communicating about excellence. Educators have learned the value of a common vocabulary to describe teaching. Because of Madeline Hunter's work, most educators know what is meant by "anticipatory set," "input and modeling," and "teaching for transfer." Now, as our understanding of teaching expands, we need a vocabulary that is correspondingly rich, one that reflects the realities of a classroom where students are engaged in constructing meaning. Such a framework is valuable for veterans as well as novices as they all strive to enhance their skills in this complex environment.

It is through serious, professional conversations about the components comprising the framework that the components are validated for any particular setting. As educators study the components and consider them within individual contexts, they can determine which components and elements are applicable and which are not. This process is critical to both enriching the professional lives of educators and to ensuring that the components used in a given setting actually do apply there. Only educators in that setting can make those determinations.

By providing an agreed-upon framework for excellence, a framework for professional practice serves to structure conversations among educators about exemplary practice. A uniform framework allows those conversations to guide novices as well as to enhance the performance of veterans.

USES FOR A FRAMEWORK

A framework for professional practice has many distinct though related uses. These are described briefly here and in greater detail in Chapter 5.

A ROAD MAP FOR NOVICES

Most professions designate a period of apprenticeship for a novice practitioner. Doctors work as interns and residents before assuming complete responsibility for patients. Attorneys work as clerks for experienced lawyers or judges, and then join a firm or an agency where they practice with attorneys experienced in the different specialty areas. Social workers employed in public agencies work under supervision before they earn a license to practice on their own.

But teachers, from the moment they are awarded their first license, are considered full members of the profession. The responsibilities of a first-year teacher are just as complex (in some situations, more so) as those of a 20-year veteran. In very few locations do teachers have an experience equivalent to the internship of a doctor or social worker; they are plunged immediately into the full responsibilities of a teacher. Some solutions, such as professional development schools that include a full-year internship, are growing in popularity. They are still rare, however, partly because of their high cost.

Given the complexity of teaching, a map of the territory is invaluable to novices, providing them with a pathway to excellence. If the map is used well and shared by mentors, it can help make the experience of becoming an accomplished professional a rewarding one.

GUIDANCE FOR EXPERIENCED PROFESSIONALS

A framework for professional practice offers the teaching profession the same definition long afforded other professions. A framework answers the questions, "What does an effective teacher know?" "What does an accomplished teacher do in the performance of her duties?" A framework is useful for all members of the profession, from those just entering, to veterans who may have lost enthusiasm for their work, to master teachers who are trying to convey their wisdom to others. Thus far, educators have lacked an agreed-upon structure that reflects new understandings of teaching and learning and offers a context for describing and discussing excellence. They rarely devote precious time to professional dialogue and sharing techniques. A framework for professional practice can provide the structure for such discussions and an opportunity for genuine professionalism.

A Structure for Focusing Improvement Efforts

When novice teachers meet with their mentors or when experienced teachers consult with their coaches or supervisors, they need a framework to determine which aspect of teaching requires their attention. They must decide which part of all the complex elements of instruction reflected in any lesson to concentrate on. A framework for professional practice can provide such a structure.

Without a framework, the structure is reduced to something the mentor, coach, or supervisor has in her head, and thus reflects the personal beliefs that individual holds about teaching, regardless of whether these have ever been made explicit. Many teachers have had the experience of conducting what they thought was a brilliant lesson only to have a principal react negatively because, for example, students were talking to one another. The teacher and the principal did not share a common understanding of what represented effective teaching.

With a framework of professional practice in hand, however, participants can conduct conversations about where to focus improvement efforts within the context of shared definitions and values. These conversations can focus on means, not ends, and they can be conducted in an environment of professional respect.

Communication with the Larger Community

An important step to enhancing the stature of educators in the family of professions is defining clearly what constitutes excellence in teaching. As long as practitioners present teaching as a mysterious art form without well-defined duties and competencies, the larger community will regard it with some mistrust. For example, many in the general public do not understand the need for teachers to attend courses and workshops: "They went to college, didn't they?" The clarity that a framework for teaching provides, including a component entitled "Growing and Developing Professionally" (Component 4e), can situate such activities squarely within the responsibilities of teaching.

A framework for professional practice has important uses in the service of teaching and learning. These uses demonstrate the framework's power to elevate professional conversations that characterize the interaction of exemplary teachers everywhere.

The Tradition of Frameworks for Teaching

Even though educators have not yet fully exploited the use of a framework to structure dialogue about teaching, the concept of a framework for professional practice derives from a long and highly respectable tradition.

Research Base

The origin of identified components of professional practice lies in a combination of Madeline Hunter's work and research in process-product and cognitive science. Hunter was one of the first educators to argue persuasively that teaching is not only an art but also a science; some demonstrable practices are clearly more effective than others. This idea was also the message of process-product research, which sought to establish relationships among certain teaching practices and enhanced student achievement, as measured by standardized tests (Wittrock 1986). The optimistic title of a book by Gage is instructive: *The Scientific Basis of the Art of Teaching* (Gage 1977). Identifying effective practices (and, in the case of Hunter, promulgating them) became the research focus in teaching during the 1970s and 1980s. Wittrock (1986) contributed to the collective knowledge base of educators by publishing the series *Handbook of Research on Teaching.*

STATE PERFORMANCE ASSESSMENT SYSTEMS

Exactly how to use the results of this research became the next challenge for educators. On a statewide basis, Georgia took the lead and used the research to create a performance assessment system that awarded a permanent license to teach in the state. Other states (particularly in the Southeast) followed suit, with systems that were modeled on Georgia's and yet had their own distinctive features. By 1990, state performance assessment systems were in place in North Carolina, Florida, and Connecticut, with others proposed (but never implemented) in Kansas and Louisiana. By 1994, New York had started using a performance assessment system for licensure, and many different versions were piloted in California.

The earliest systems tended to identify specific teaching

behaviors (e.g., writing learning objectives on the board) supposedly derived from the research on effective teaching, and to rate teachers on their demonstration of these practices. The later systems, particularly in Connecticut, adopted a more complex view of teaching and considered the quality of a teacher's judgment. For example, a Connecticut competency states that teachers should be able to "formulate meaningful questions about the subject matter." All state systems rely on the decisions that assessors make; the assessors, therefore, must be trained and certified to make both professional and legally defensible judgments in their assessments of teaching.

PRAXIS III: CLASSROOM PERFORMANCE ASSESSMENTS

The performance assessment tradition was continued by Educational Testing Service in 1987, when it announced that it was creating a "new generation" of teacher licensing tests. Called The PRAXIS Series: Professional Assessments for Beginning Teachers, the new assessments are intended to replace the widely used National Teacher Examination (NTE). The final phase of The PRAXIS Series is PRAXIS III: Classroom Performance Assessments. PRAXIS III uses the performance assessment of new teachers in their classrooms as part of the process to grant a permanent license. Trained and certified assessors conduct classroom observations and semistructured interviews with first- and second-year teachers. A nonlicensing outgrowth of PRAXIS III: Classroom Performance Assessments, called Pathwise, is now available for teacher training institutions and school districts.

OTHER NATIONAL FRAMEWORKS

Nationally prominent organizations have proposed sets of standards primarily for student teachers. For example, the Interstate New Teacher Assessment and Support Consortium (INTASC) developed standards to be compatible with those of the National Board for Professional Teaching Standards (NBPTS). This combination has served as the foundation of standard-setting efforts in about 20 states. A correlation of the framework offered here and the INTASC standards is shown in Figure 1.2 (see pp. 10–11). Similarly, the National Association of State Directors of Teacher Education and Certification (NAS-DTEC) and the National Council of Accreditation of Teacher Education (NCATE) have both proposed standards for beginning teacher competencies. The standards are intended to guide colleges in the design or redesign of teacher education programs.

NATIONAL BOARD FOR PROFESSIONAL TEACHING STANDARDS

The latest player on the standards scene is NBPTS. It was created in 1988 following the publication of the report *A Nation Prepared: Teachers for the 21st Century,* from the Carnegie Foundation for the Advancement of Teaching. NBPTS was formed to offer teachers the equivalent of advanced board certification in medicine. Just as a medical doctor earns an initial license to practice medicine and then passes a test for board certification in, for example, pediatrics, the theory of the national board is that teachers should be able to earn advanced certification in any of the subject matter areas or levels, for example, early childhood or high school mathematics. NBPTS plans to offer over 30 separate certificates to teachers on a voluntary basis.

PARALLEL DEVELOPMENTS IN STUDENT ASSESSMENT

The movement towards a framework for teaching has had, of course, parallel developments in student learning and assessment. Many states have embarked on a program of performance assessment of student learning in ways that better reflect the complex learning they intend for their students and that more authentically represent the application of school knowledge. Now used in Maryland, Vermont, Kentucky, and elsewhere, and under development in North Carolina, Oregon, and Washington State, these systems involve establishing curriculum frameworks and standards, benchmarks of student performance at different levels, and performance assessments aligned to these benchmarks. They also frequently engage teachers as trained assessors to evaluate student work.

BY-PRODUCTS OF THE MOVEMENT TOWARD FRAMEWORKS

The use of frameworks, whether to define and describe exemplary student performance, or to define and describe excellence in teaching, has produced powerful side effects. Even though the original purpose was to show accountability, practitioners themselves have enjoyed enormous benefits.

It has long been recognized that articulating clear standards for student learning, illustrated by examples of exemplary student work, enhances the quality of that work and students' sense of purpose. Teachers have discovered that when they are clear to students about criteria to evaluate a science project, for example, students are far more focused, and the resulting projects are of higher quality than

Figure 1.2

Correlation of the INTASC Standards with the Framework for Teaching Components

INTASC Standard	Description of Teacher Performance	Framework Component	Description of Teacher Performance
Principle 1	Understands the central concepts, tools of inquiry, and structure of the disciplines taught; creates learning experiences to make them meaningful to students.	1a 1e 3c	Demonstrates knowledge of content and pedagogy. Designs coherent instruction. Engages students in learning.
Principle 2	Understands how children learn and develop; provides learning opportunities that support their development.	1b 1c 1f 3b 3c	Demonstrates knowledge of students. Selects instructional goals. Assesses student learning. Uses questioning and discussion techniques. Engages students in learning.
Principle 3	Understands how students differ in their approaches to learning; creates instructional opportunities adapted to diverse learners.	1b 1e 2a 2b 3b to 3e	Demonstrates knowledge of students. Designs coherent instruction. Creates an environment of respect and rapport. Establishes a culture for learning. Instruction Domain.
Principle 4	Understands and uses variety of instructional strategies.	1d 1e 3b to 3e	Demonstrates knowledge of resources. Designs coherent instruction. Instruction Domain.
Principle 5	Creates a learning environment that encourages positive social interaction, active engagement in learning, and self-motivation.	1e 2a 2b 2c 2d 2e 3c	Designs coherent instruction. Creates an environment of respect and rapport. Establishes a culture for learning. Manages classroom procedures. Manages student behavior. Organizes physical space. Engages students in learning.

Figure 1.2

Correlation of the INTASC Standards with the Framework for Teaching Components *(continued)*

INTASC Standard	Description of Teacher Performance	Framework Component	Description of Teacher Performance
Principle 6	Uses knowledge of communication techniques to foster active inquiry, collaboration, and supportive interaction.	2a 3a 3b 3c	Creates an environment of respect and rapport. Communicates clearly and accurately. Uses questioning and discussion techniques. Engages students in learning.
Principle 7	Plans instruction based on knowledge of subject matter, students, the community, and curriculum goals.	1a to 1e 3c 3e	Planning and Preparation Domain. Engages students in learning. Demonstrates flexibility and responsiveness.
Principle 8	Understands and uses formal and informal assessment strategies.	1b 1f 3d 3e 4a 4b 4c	Demonstrates knowledge of students. Assesses student learning. Provides feedback to students. Demonstrates flexibility and responsiveness. Reflects on teaching. Maintains accurate records. Communicates with families.
Principle 9	Reflects on teaching.	4a 4d 4e	Reflects on teaching. Contributes to the school and district. Grows and develops professionally.
Principle 10	Fosters relationships with colleagues, parents, and agencies in the larger community.	1d 4c 4d 4f	Demonstrates knowledge of resources. Communicates with families. Contributes to the school and district. Shows professionalism.

without the criteria. Furthermore, students who might have believed that high grades were beyond their reach now see clearly how to achieve the grades.

The same phenomenon is at work with a framework for teaching. When teachers are beginning their careers, the challenge of becoming a skilled practitioner is daunting. Teaching is so complex and its various components so intertwined that many novices feel overwhelmed. A framework for teaching offers a structure to assess a teacher's practice and to organize improvement efforts. In addition, to implement teacher mentoring and licensing systems or to certify teachers under NBPTS, many educators must be trained as mentors or assessors. During such training, practitioners must think seriously about teaching, learn to recognize the various components in different contexts, and as a consequence, reflect deeply on their own practice. This reflection, conducted in a professional and supportive environment and in the service of another purpose (becoming a mentor or certified assessor), is an enriching experience. Practitioners report that the experience is their first opportunity in many years to discuss *teaching* seriously—in its complex entirety—with respected colleagues.

CHALLENGES

Using performance assessment presents many challenges, whether the goal is to evaluate teachers for licensure or to evaluate student learning for state accountability. We need to understand what these challenges are because they are relevant to the ways this framework can, and should, be used.

Validity

How do educators know that a given framework is valid, that it incorporates what is important about teaching? Educators can choose from many frameworks to use for discussion. The one they select must reflect their own assumptions and beliefs about teaching and learning. The framework for professional practice presented here is based on one developed from a solid research base (see Appendix); it also reflects important assumptions and beliefs (see Chapter 2). If these are convincing to educators, they will probably find that the framework provides useful guidance.

But we should also remember that for school and district use (as distinct from state use to license beginning teachers), the validity of a framework derives from the professional conversations that accompany its introduction into a school or district. Each component will be manifested differently in different contexts—8th graders, after all, are very different from kindergartners—and some components or elements may not apply in some settings. Validation of this type can only occur at the local level in the collegial environment that accompanies professional conversation.

Reliability

Many large-scale assessment systems have found that with adequate training, independent assessors can make comparable judgments about, for example, a student's writing or the way a teacher conducts a class. Such systems have shown high levels of interrater agreement, which is considered critical to demonstrate the reliability of the system. This is principally a training issue; for individuals to make similar independent judgments, they must operate from a common vision and similar definitions of the evaluation criteria.

Of course, reliability can be increased by focusing on trivial, "low-inference" criteria. For example, if a criterion relates to whether a teacher writes the lesson objectives on the board, independent observers can easily agree on whether the teacher has done it. For more substantive criteria, such as the skilled use of questioning and discussion strategies (Component 3b), informed, independent observers can reasonably disagree to some extent.

Reliability is essential in a high-stakes environment. If an individual's teaching license depends on the results of several classroom observations, the assessors' judgments must be reliable. But if a framework for teaching is used within a school or district primarily for mentoring and coaching, with support and professional dialogue as the principal purpose, then interrater agreement is less critical.

Cost

Cost is another challenge. State licensing systems, NBPTS, and the state student assessment systems are all accompanied by a high price tag for development and, more important, operation. All features are expensive, from training assessors, to conducting assessments (for state licensing systems) or scoring sessions (for NBPTS and student assessment systems), to designing and implementing the information management systems. Sometimes cost has led to cancelling or scaling back systems.

Schools or districts using a framework for professional practice do not face the difficulty of high cost encountered by large-scale state or national systems. To make use of a framework for teaching, all participants must become familiar with the system and must incorporate its use with beginning or veteran teachers. These are functions that most schools or districts would implement as part of their mentoring, coaching, and professional development programs. In other words, using the framework for professional practice need not require an additional commitment of funds; it can simply improve the quality of a school or district's existing programs for improvement and renewal.

The components of professional practice are part of a long tradition of applying standards to both student learning and the complex role of teaching. Despite challenges, the benefits, particularly for school and district use, are enormous.

2 FEATURES AND ASSUMPTIONS OF THE FRAMEWORK

The framework for professional practice represents all aspects of a teacher's responsibilities that are reflected in daily work. It derives from the most recent theoretical and empirical research about teaching and aims to apply to all situations. This chapter describes general features of the framework and the assumptions upon which the system is based.

FEATURES

The framework for teaching embodies a number of features that ensure its applicability to a wide range of instructional settings.

COMPREHENSIVE

The framework is comprehensive, referring not only to what occurs in the classroom, of course, but also to what happens outside its walls:

• Planning for instruction and reflecting on next steps.

• Interacting with colleagues in the faculty lounge, on school and district committees, and in pursuit of instructional improvement.

• Communicating with parents and the larger community.

The framework makes it clear that a teacher's job is far more than what happens in a classroom by acknowledging that other types of work contribute significantly to a teacher's success with students. Such work includes the following:

• What occurs in a teacher's head, such as knowledge of content and ways to organize that knowledge to convey it to students.

• How a teacher reflects on student learning and makes plans to improve that learning.

• How a teacher interacts with other players in the educational environment, such as parents, colleagues, and the business community.

The 22 components of the framework for teaching are organized to encompass the primary areas of teaching responsibility: planning and preparation, classroom environment, instruction, and professional responsibilities. Although instruction (Domain 3) is the centerpiece of a teacher's role, it cannot successfully be carried out if work in the other areas is neglected or performed inadequately. For example, students will not be engaged in learning content if the teacher does not have a deep understanding of that content and how to organize it for learning, if the classroom environment is chaotic or disrespectful, or if the teacher is not an active player with other stakeholders (parents, colleagues, and the larger community) in the educational enterprise.

PUBLIC

One of the main principles of the framework is that it is publicly known. Particularly if it is used for supervision, there is no place for a "gotcha" mentality.

Implications for promulgating the framework are profound. First and most important, such action puts meaningful discussion surrounding the components in the hands of those who must use them—namely, teachers. Decisions on the applicability of each element to a given situation must be made by those who are most familiar with that situation—namely, teachers.

Second, when a framework is public, discussion becomes an important vehicle for professional development. Dialogue that centers on the framework and how the different components are revealed in different contexts becomes a powerful vehicle for meaningful discussion about the enhancement of teaching.

Third, if the framework is used for mentoring or supervision, it can help a teacher select improvement goals. Through self-reflection and analysis, a teacher can identify the components on which to concentrate, with a mentor or supervisor available as a coach. If the framework is kept secret, this opportunity would not be available.

GENERIC

It is well known—certainly by teachers—that every teaching situation is unique. Each day, in each classroom, a particular combination of factors defines the events that occur. The personalities of both teacher and students interacting with one another and with the content result in a unique environment. Many educators believe that because of this uniqueness, there can be no generic framework that defines teaching. They point to the systematic differences in technique between teaching mathematics and foreign language; they cite the different approaches to learning exhibited by 1st graders and high school sophomores. And they point out that the makeup of a class, for example, whether the students are from urban or rural areas or whether student cultural traditions match those of the school, heavily influences the decisions a teacher makes about organizing the content and engaging students in learning.

And yet beneath the unique features of each situation are powerful commonalties. It is these common themes that the framework taps. For example, in every classroom, an effective teacher creates an environment of respect and rapport (Component 2a). How that is done and what is specifically observed are very different in a kindergarten class and a high school biology class, in an urban and a rural setting. But the underlying construct is the same: Students feel respected by the teacher and their peers; they believe that the teacher *cares* about them and their learning. Similarly, techniques to engage students in writing a persuasive essay are fundamentally different from those to engage students in a conceptual understanding of place value. But in both cases, students are deeply engaged in the task at hand and take pride in their work. The framework for professional practice captures this engagement and pride.

The framework applies to virtually every setting. It describes those aspects of teaching that occur in some form in every context. How each component is demonstrated—the specific actions a teacher or students may take—will vary in different situations, as described earlier. And although some components are more important in some contexts than in others, the components themselves apply to every setting.

Elements of a component, however, may not apply in all contexts. For example, Component 2c (managing classroom procedures) contains an element about the supervision of volunteers and paraprofessionals. Clearly, if a teacher is not fortunate enough—and many are not—to have such assistance, this element does not apply. But the component itself, including the other elements of classroom procedures—managing instructional groups, transitions, materials, and noninstructional duties—is present in every classroom setting.

NOT A CHECKLIST OF SPECIFIC TEACHING BEHAVIORS

Many early efforts to establish frameworks for teaching identified specific actions teachers should take. These efforts were based on the assumption that if teachers performed all the required elements, student learning would increase. Many of these so-called "teaching behaviors" derive from research on effective teaching and were thus grounded in the process-product research. In this research, approaches to teaching were compared for their effectiveness. It was argued that if students in one class scored higher on, or made greater gains in, standardized tests (the product), then the approaches used in that class (the process) must be superior. Such considerations guided many of the early state assessment systems for teacher licensure (e.g., those in Georgia and North Carolina).

Because this research is based on standardized test measures, many teachers believe that such a narrow conceptualization of teaching is not applicable to the complexity of their setting. Some found that they adopted the required behaviors (e.g., writing their learning objectives on the board) only on the day they were being observed. Such dog and pony shows have contributed to teachers' impression that their profession is not a true one and that they are not afforded the respect of autonomous decision making, a hallmark of professionalism in other domains.

Moreover, the foundation of such frameworks, namely the process-product research itself, has been strongly criticized in recent years. Its main weakness is its reliance on standardized tests as the measure of effectiveness. Focusing on low-level bits of information and isolated skills, these tests tend to reward instruction oriented to such learning. This learning has been characterized by a superficial treatment of many topics, which are presented through a few, specific teaching behaviors.

The framework for professional practice, on the other hand, provides a structure within which educators can situate their actions. The components are grounded in the assumption that even though good teachers may accomplish many of the same things, they do not achieve them in the same way. Therefore, a list of specific behaviors is not appropriate. Rather, what is needed is a set of commonalties underlying the actions, with the recognition that specific actions will and should vary, depending on the context and the individual. These common themes represent the effects achieved—for example, providing feedback to students (Component 3d)—rather than the specific actions taken to provide such feedback.

NOT AN ENDORSEMENT OF A PARTICULAR TEACHING STYLE

Educators have experienced another difficulty with previous attempts to develop frameworks for teaching. Prior frameworks appeared to reflect a particular approach to instruction. As noted earlier, such an approach seems to violate the very notion of professionalism. Although the idea of dictating an approach was well motivated, stemming from the promulgation of a "scientific basis for the art of teaching" (Gage 1977), this rationale seemed to take the position that the same approach would be effective for all types of learning with all types of students.

Partly to respond to the overly prescriptive models presented in the early 1980s, many educators and researchers delved into the field of learning and teaching styles. Based on their research, they argued that just as students bring different strengths to aid their learning, so teachers have different strengths, which are expressed as their "style"; none are better than any other. Where one teacher may be nurturing, another may be firm; where one teacher lectures, another may use small groups.

The framework for teaching is grounded in the belief that both positions are inadequate. Indeed, selecting instructional approaches rests absolutely with a teacher; this decision is a critical element of professionalism. Not all choices, however, are effective; not all are equally appropriate. Decisions about instructional strategies and learning activities involve matching the desired outcomes of a lesson or a unit (i.e., what the students are to learn) with the approaches selected. Not only should the instructional goals be worthwhile, but the methods and materials chosen should be appropriate for those goals and help students attain them.

What is required, then, is that teachers have a repertoire of strategies from which they can select a suitable one for a given purpose. No single approach will be effective in every situation, for each set of instructional goals, or with all individuals or groups of students. These choices and decisions represent the heart of professionalism. And for many educators, adding to the repertoire is their primary purpose in attending workshops and inservice sessions and taking university courses. Teachers know that they are never finished acquiring strategies to suit different purposes. They can always gain new insights and new approaches to meet their (and their students') instructional purposes.

One framework that is helpful in analyzing different approaches and organizational patterns is provided in Figure 2.1 (see p. 19), which identifies four ways of grouping students for instruction. In the first pattern, students are together in a large group and involved in a single activity that a teacher or another student leads. This activity can be a lecture, discussion, or student presentation. In the second pattern, a teacher works with a small group of students, while other students work alone or independently in small groups. This pattern is the basic "reading group" organization. In the third pattern, students work in small groups, and the teacher circulates to assist as needed. Science teachers frequently use this organization when students are completing a laboratory assignment. In the last pattern, students work alone, with the teacher circulating or conducting conferences

with individual students. Many types of tasks fall into this grouping, from worksheets, to writing assignments, to problem sets.

The figure also describes different levels of student initiative. The levels range from low (e.g., answering questions from a teacher or textbook), to moderate (e.g., writing an essay on one of several topics that a teacher has proposed), to high (e.g., devising an experiment to test a theory a student has generated). Therefore, a teacher's lecture or a student presentation is an example of (A); a student-led discussion on a topic the class selects is an example of (B). A teacher meeting with a group of students to discuss a book that they have selected from a range of choices the teacher has offered is an example of (C); a science lab in which students are following an established procedure illustrates (D). Students completing a worksheet assignment by the teacher fits (E); students writing an essay on a topic of their own choosing is an example of (F).

No arrangement is superior to the others; all can promote high-quality learning. At any time in a classroom, students will be working individually or in a group, and they will be engaged in a task at some level of initiative. They may be working in several different group patterns and at different levels of initiative in succession.

Which approach a teacher selects depends on both the content to be learned and the students' age and preferred approach. The teacher is the person most knowledgeable about those elements. Another professional, however, when informed of the content and the students, may have suggestions about other approaches that might have been as effective, or perhaps more so. But the discussion is about the *appropriateness* of different choices; there are no right and wrong answers.

Figure 2.1

Approaches to Classroom Organization and Instruction

Grouping Pattern	LEVEL OF STUDENT INITIATIVE		
	Low	Moderate	High
Teacher or student leads large-group presentation.	(A)		(B)
Teacher works with small groups; other students work alone or in small groups.		(C)	
Students work in small groups; teacher circulates.	(D)		
Students work alone; teacher monitors.	(E)		(F)

The framework for professional practice does not endorse any particular teaching style for all teachers; it does, however, enable educators to engage in conversations about the appropriateness of choices made at many points in a lesson or unit. No one approach is a "one size fits all." But some approaches will be better suited to certain purposes than others. Making good and defensible choices is the hallmark of a professional educator.

DEPENDENT ON CONTEXT

The components depend on context for their specific manifestation. In fact, identification of student and teacher actions that illustrate the components in different contexts is the principal way that educators can develop an understanding of them.

For example, Component 1c is "Selecting Instructional Goals." Its elements specify that these goals should be (1) of value, reflecting important learning in a discipline; (2) clearly stated and unambiguously related to student learning, rather than consisting simply of activities; (3) suitable for diverse learners in a class; and (4) balanced as appropriate between different types of learning, such as knowledge and skills. The component applies to all contexts—all educators select instructional goals for their units and lessons. Even if instructional materials provide goals, teachers must still determine which are most suitable for their students.

For a unit on place value in mathematics, a 3rd grade teacher might include the following instructional goals for students:

- Read two-digit and three-digit numerals.
- Create representations of two-digit and three-digit numbers with manipulative materials.
- Add and subtract two-digit numbers with and without regrouping.
- Solve problems involving two-digit addition and subtraction.
- Explain to others either orally or in writing why a particular method is correct.

These goals can be analyzed according to the elements of Component 1c: value, clarity, suitability for diverse students, and balance.

Instructional goals for an 8th grade science teacher, a physical education teacher with a 4th grade class, and an English teacher of Advanced Placement English literature will be different. But they can all be analyzed for their value, clarity, suitability, and balance; they can all illustrate the elements of Component 1c.

The same is true for the other components. In particular, the components in Domain 2 (the classroom environment) are highly dependent on context. For example, details of how a teacher organizes the physical environment (Component 2e) and develops a culture for learning (Component 2b) are influenced by the nature of the school, age and developmental level of the students, and the general approach the teacher takes. Despite these differences, all teachers try to create a physical environment conducive to learning and develop cultures for learning.

When mentors and coaches observe colleagues' classrooms, they must beware of imposing their own styles on what they see. The question is not, "Has this teacher established a physical environment in the same way I would do it?" but rather, "Given this teacher's situation—age of the students and nature of the school and class—has this teacher successfully established a physical environment conducive to learning? What suggestions can I make, *given this context and given this teacher's general approach?*" Thus, although the components apply in some form to all contexts, their manifestations vary greatly in ways that make them appropriate to diverse settings.

CAN BE DEMONSTRATED IN DIVERSE WAYS

The components are not all demonstrated in the classroom. Of course, Domain 2 (the classroom environment) and Domain 3 (instruction) are demonstrated principally through a teacher's interaction with students. But many other components, including all of Domain 4 (professional responsibilities), are manifested in the inter-

actions a teacher has with families; colleagues, both within the school and district and in larger groups, such as professional organizations and university classes; and the community of business and civic leaders. Domain 1 (planning and preparation) is revealed through a teacher's plans for instruction. Although the success of those plans is only fully demonstrated in the classroom and primarily through what happens in Domain 3 (instruction), the success of the instructional design *as a design* is revealed through the unit and lesson plans.

Teachers can also demonstrate many components through materials they create and interpret (see Chapter 4 for further explanation). For example, a class or homework assignment, showing a few samples of student work, sheds light on the level of student engagement in learning (Component 3c); logs of contact with families can document Component 4c (communicating with families); and logs of committee meetings and school events can document Component 4d (contributing to the school and district).

Some components are not directly observable and must be inferred. For example, Component 2d concerns the management of student behavior. One element is expectations, meaning that all students understand the standards of conduct and have participated if possible in establishing those standards. If a mentor or coach visits a class in December, the standards will probably have been established, so they may not be discussed during a lesson. The observer, however, may be able to infer—perhaps from displayed material or by the interaction of students with their peers and teacher—whether such standards have been successfully established. What is *observed* is behavior—both students' and teacher's. But what is *inferred* relates to the standards of conduct established in the class.

The framework for teaching has features that make it applicable to all teaching situations:

- Comprehensive, public, and generic.
- Not a checklist of teaching behaviors.
- Not an endorsement of a particular teaching style or organizational structure.
- Dependent on context.
- Can be demonstrated in diverse ways.

UNDERLYING ASSUMPTIONS

Whether for student learning or professional practice, frameworks reflect the priorities of the people who assemble them. Frameworks also represent the orientation of their creators. For example, National Council of Teachers of Mathematics (NCTM) standards for student learning adopt a problem-solving orientation to mathematics. A curriculum consistent with those standards emphasizes problem solving in all areas of mathematics; therefore, instructional practices that cultivate problem solving are more consistent with the standards than those that promote rote recall of procedures.

This framework for teaching is based on specific assumptions and orientations about teaching and learning. The next section explains these assumptions.

GROUNDED IN RESEARCH

To the greatest extent possible, the framework for teaching is grounded in a body of research that seeks to identify principles of effective practice and classroom organization. Such principles maximize student learning and promote student engagement. Some of this research is empirical; that is, it is grounded in experience, with formal research data to support it. Some, however, is theoretical; that is, it is not (yet) or cannot be supported by empirical data. In these cases, the framework is based on recommendations from theoretical research on cognition and on practices that are recommended but not yet rigorously tested in classrooms.

Ideally, we would search the research literature for studies evaluating different instructional approaches that help students reach the desired educational goals. Unfortunately, given the changing nature of goals in education today, the imperfect nature of assessment, and the difficulties of social research, few such studies exist. All the ingredients of the research design—the educational goals, the measures or indicators of goal achievement, and the control of extraneous variables—present difficulties.

One difficulty is the nature of educational goals. Many policy leaders and educators now agree that our educational goals for the past 100 years are inadequate for students to meet the challenges of today and tomorrow. Traditionally, schools emphasized rote learning, memorization of facts and procedures, and recall of information, with little emphasis on conceptual understanding and reasoning. The global economy, the revolution in information technology, and the rapidly changing nature of the workplace are all strong incentives for schools to produce graduates, all of whom—not merely an elite—are knowledgeable, flexible in thinking and understanding, and capable of understanding complex ideas.

Many new state and district goals are attempts to respond to these demands. But consensus on the goals has not yet occurred, nor has much progress been made on translating them into concrete curriculums for schools and teachers.

A second difficulty concerns assessment. To conduct educational research, educators must know whether students have met the instructional goals and whether one approach was more effective than another in meeting those goals. The choice of assessment measures then becomes critical to the research design.

Traditionally, assessment measures used in educational research have been multiple-choice tests in which students select the best answer. Educators and researchers have pointed out the inadequacy of such tests, particularly for the new generation of educational goals. Traditional standardized tests are fairly reliable in assessing bits of information, low-level knowledge, and routinized procedures. But they are unsatisfactory for assessing conceptual understanding. For example, a thorough understanding of "buoyancy" is different from the ability to select its correct definition from a list of choices.

Valid and reliable assessment measures are urgently needed for the new generation of instructional goals. Until researchers have these measures, they cannot conduct credible research on the effectiveness of alternative approaches.

A third difficulty with educational research concerns control over extraneous variables. Clean research design requires that any experimental technique tried with a group of students be compared with an alternate (presumably conventional) approach. Insofar as possible, both the students and the teachers involved in the research must be comparable.

These requirements present enormous difficulty in educational as well as in other social research. First, teachers who volunteer to try a new approach are usually greater risk-takers than their colleagues, who do not want to attempt it. And if teachers are assigned randomly to the experimental and control groups, some teachers will be required to use approaches that they do not believe are effective. Therefore, teachers who volunteer to try a new approach may reflect a systematic bias, and the results will reflect this bias as well.

Second, controlling student populations for extraneous variables is notoriously difficult. Students are enormously diverse, as every teacher knows. They arrive at school with a full range of academic preparation, interests, cultural norms, and preferred approaches to learning. Any given technique is bound to be more effective with some students than with others. To make sound conclusions from educational research, then, studies must involve large numbers of students and must assume that there are no systematic biases in the assignment of different students to different experimental groups.

* * *

All these factors combine to produce a research environment that is far from ideal. The ingredients required for clean research studies—educational goals, assessment measures, and control over extraneous variables—are compromised. Consequently, hard, empirical research in education is scanty—at least today, with our limited assessment measures and our evolving goals.

In their efforts to advance the research agenda beyond their process-product findings, educators and researchers seek clarity on instructional goals and then challenge practitioners to specify what excellence on those goals will look like in different contexts. Researchers and practitioners use this information in qualitative research, which provides hints of exemplary practice, to reach tentative conclusions. For the moment, it is the best we can do.

But given these limitations and caveats, the framework for professional practice derives as much as possible from sound educational research. In those cases where empirical research has not yet been conducted, it derives from recommendations of experts in curriculum, instruction, and assessment and draws extensively on the most current theoretical research literature and writings of leading authorities.

A New Paradigm for Learning and Teaching

Educators, researchers, and policymakers concur that the traditional view of learning, focused on knowledge and procedures of low cognitive challenge and the regurgitation of superficial understanding, does not meet the demands of the present and future. Competitive industries in the 21st century will be those whose workers can solve complex problems and design more efficient techniques to accomplish work. To be sure, much basic knowledge is important for students to understand. But deep, conceptual understanding—knowledge that lasts longer than the time it takes for a student to pass a test—is also needed. How that kind of knowledge is acquired and how to develop the cognitive energy needed for understanding and processing information are at the heart of the new paradigm.

Educators and policymakers have been speaking recently of constructivism and a constructivist approach to learning (and therefore teaching). During the past few years, this orientation has become *de rigueur* in educational circles and is reflected in the new curriculum standards begun by NCTM and followed by other professional organizations and many states. We must recognize, however, that this movement is not new. Constructivism stems from a long and respected tradition in cognitive psychology, especially the writings of Dewey, Vygotsky, and Piaget. Since the early 20th century, these cognitive approaches have competed for attention with the more behaviorist orientation of Skinner, Bereiter, and their followers in the back-to-basics movement of the 1970s.

So what is the constructivist approach, and why does it represent a new paradigm? Constructivism holds that people's understanding of any concept depends entirely on their mental construction of that concept—that is, their experience in deriving that concept for themselves. Teachers can, of course, guide the process, but students must undertake and manage the process of developing an understanding for themselves. The constructivist approach makes explicit that different individuals, depending on their experiences, knowledge, *and their cognitive structures at the time* will understand a given presentation differently. Research shows that people remember an experience based on what their pre-existing knowledge and cognitive structures allow them to absorb—regardless of a teacher's intentions or the quality of an explanation.

An example of the influence of cognitive structures is how students learn science, particularly when the "official" explanation of a principle violates students' intuitive understanding. For example, most elementary and middle school students are convinced that their eyes see objects. In fact, our eyes see light that is reflected from objects. This fact can easily be proven to students—and students can prove it to themselves—by looking at a stick in water, where it appears bent. A clear explanation of the scientifically correct theory by itself would be insufficient to convince students that their understanding is inadequate. Instead, they must experience situations that cannot be explained by their conception of light and vision. A teacher's responsibility becomes one of arranging for students' misconceptions to be confronted by conflicting evidence.

To use a more practical example, suppose a teacher wants students to understand the concept of pi, a mathematical concept equal to approximately 3.14. The teacher can make a presentation on pi, saying that it is a constant equal to about 3.14 and giving examples of how it is used.

To teach the concept of pi in a constructivist manner, the teacher needs to engage students in understanding it in their own way and primarily in their own time. For example, the teacher can present students with many round objects and ask them to measure their diameters and circumferences. The students analyze the data, perhaps using a graph or making a table. The teacher then challenges students to discern the patterns reflected in the data. The students observe a pattern in the data and recognize, possibly with teacher guidance, that the graph they have made is a straight line or that the circumference divided by the diameter is a constant. The slope of the line and the constant are both a little greater than 3 and represent what mathematicians call pi. Only when students have engaged in such an investigation can they be said to truly *understand* pi.

The goal of having students understand pi is a traditional one. Pi figures into the formulas for calculating areas in the most traditional presentations of mathematics. But this way of understanding pi is constructivist. A teacher using this approach recognizes that if students are to obtain a conceptual understanding of the concept, they must do much of the intellectual work themselves; they must see the patterns and derive the relationships. Such an approach also suggests that students can acquire an understanding of pi in many ways. Many instructional sequences can achieve the goal. Within a single class, some students may use the graphing method, while others calculate the quotients. Others may devise yet another method of investigation. But all will notice patterns in the data and will derive the relationship between the two sets of numbers.

Nothing in this approach is particularly new or controversial; teachers have used these types of techniques for years. Such teaching tends to place demands on time, however, since students require more time to construct a concept than to be simply told about it. These considerations have led to the "less is more" slogan of the Coalition of Essential Schools. Schools in this network choose which topics and concepts in the curriculum are critical and eliminate some that are not. What is lost in time is more than made up for in student engagement and energy. When students are constructing their own understanding, they cannot be lethargic or alienated from the process. They must invest energy and commitment. Moreover, their learning is permanent. Once students have derived pi, they tend to remember it. So while fewer topics may be covered, more is actually learned.

It is important to keep in mind that construction of knowledge is not the same as physical involvement with manipulative materials. So-called "hands-on" learning may or may not be constructivist. Students can follow directions as mindlessly when using physical objects as they can when completing a worksheet. In a constructivist approach, students engage their minds in understanding; they must be "minds-on." Although in many situations, physical involvement with real objects aids this process, physical involvement provides no guarantee that students will be mentally engaged.

Of course, not all valuable learning is constructivist. Other types of learning, such as rote learning, have an important role, too. The instructional challenge is in knowing when to do which. To take another example from mathematics, suppose the goal is for students to understand the concept of addition, which is grounded in developmental structures of number conservation and additive composition. They must construct the understanding that each time 5 and 3 are added together in any order and using any representation, the answer is always 8. But once the concept is thoroughly understood, memorizing the addition facts can proceed by rote. Patterns can help the learning process, but at the end of the day, students should know the facts.

The constructivist approach has important implications for teaching and for the role of a teacher in student learning. When considering an environment where students are constructing their own understanding, educators may conclude that there is nothing for a teacher to do. On the contrary, a teacher's role in a constructivist class is no less than in a traditional one. It is simply different. Teaching no longer focuses solely on making presentations (although those are still sometimes appropriate) or assigning questions and exercises. Instead, teaching focuses on designing activities and assignments—many of them framed as problem solving—that can engage students in constructing important knowledge.

As an example, consider a middle school class learning about the Civil War. In a traditional class, a teacher may ask students to write a report on a battle, such as the Second Battle of Bull Run. And typically, the reports will include barely disguised encyclopedia accounts of the battle. Instead of a report, however, suppose the teacher asks students to imagine that they are soldiers (either Union or Confederate) in the battle and to write a letter home. Students will need not only to learn information about the battle from as many sources as possible but also to *do something* with the information. They will have to coordinate versions from different perspectives, draw their own conclusions, and personalize the information.

The framework for teaching is grounded in the constructivist approach. It assumes that the primary goal of education is to engage students in constructing important knowledge and that it is each teacher's responsibility, using the resources at hand, to accomplish that goal. Naturally, this is a highly complex view of teaching, one that recognizes the many decisions that must be made daily to realize such a vision. But the framework also takes the position that to meet the needs of our citizens of the future, nothing less will do.

THE PURPOSEFUL NATURE OF TEACHING

Another important assumption underlying the framework for teaching is that instructional decisions are purposeful. Activities and assignments are not chosen merely because they are fun. They are selected or designed because they serve the instructional goals of the teacher, as guided by the students' interests and strengths.

This focus on purpose sets this framework apart from many other teaching frameworks. Generally, teachers are asked to demonstrate that their students are on-task or that students treat one another with respect. But teachers are rarely asked to explain the reasons for being on-task or for behaving respectfully. The questions that should be asked are, "What instructional purpose is being served?" "Is this instructional purpose worthwhile?" Even instructional practices that are widely regarded as good, such as integrated, thematic units, may not have a significant purpose.

In the framework for teaching, purpose is central. Component 1c (selecting instructional goals) casts a long shadow over the entire framework. The instructional goals must themselves be valuable and suitable to the students. In addition, the instructional methods, proposed assessment techniques, and teacher's reflection on the lesson must address the instructional goals. Do the activities and materials serve to achieve the instructional purpose that the teacher has established? Will the assessment techniques actually assess student achievement of the goals, and will they respect both the content and the processes inherent in the goals?

A COMMUNITY OF LEARNERS

A consequence of the new paradigm of learning and teaching is the idea of a community of learners. This idea suggests that a teacher is not the sole source of knowledge; students also participate in generating and sharing understanding. The teacher and students together become a learning community in which everyone's contributions are valued.

Some educators suggest that in a community of learners, students determine both what is studied and how it should be approached. In this view, which might be appropriate in a graduate-level seminar, students take total control of the educational environment. Such an orientation, however, is not suitable in an elementary or high school, where students are young and inexperienced; there is much that they are encountering for the first time. They generally do not have enough knowledge about the Civil War, for example, to know what questions are important to ask. A teacher needs to create the overall plan.

A class where a teacher is clearly setting the agenda, however, can still become a community of learners. For example, as students learn more about the Civil War, they will—and should be encouraged to—formulate questions that the teacher may not have considered. Depending on the teacher's instructional goals, such questions may be suitable for investigation. And once students have gained some insight, even on questions the teacher has posed, they are in a position to share those insights with other students, entering into a dialogue about the subject with their peers and resource people, which the teacher monitors and facilitates but does not direct.

The framework is clear about a teacher's role in creating an environment for productive learning. Setting the broad agenda is part of a teacher's responsibility. The environment, however, can consist of a learning community. In such a community, the lines between teacher and learner become somewhat blurred; individuals move back and forth across that line in the course of their work, without relinquishing responsibility. A teacher is not afraid to acknowledge when he does not know a particular fact, and he recognizes and specifically utilizes student contributions to the production of knowledge.

THE ROLE OF APPROPRIATENESS

As already discussed earlier in this chapter, the framework does not require that certain teaching behaviors be used. Rather, it asks educators, "What combination of particular activities, materials, and methods are *appropriate* to a situation, given a set of instructional goals (the purpose) and an actual group of students?"

There is clearly no single right answer to that question. Many possible combinations will work, and the role of an educator should not be to impose her choices on others. But conversations among colleagues about appropriateness are valuable and can benefit both parties. Of course, such conversations draw on knowledge of the curriculum, students, and environment. They challenge educators to make and discuss professional judgments. They also encourage an open mind toward other approaches to the same set of purposes.

THE NATURE OF PROFESSIONALISM

Teaching has struggled for some time with its role in the world of the professions. Generally speaking, it is neither as prestigious nor as well paid as other occupations, such as medicine, accounting, architecture, and law, which are openly acknowledged as professions. Teaching has been treated and, to some degree, has treated itself as a job, with almost an assembly-line mentality.

Part of the new paradigm of learning and teaching recognizes the complexity and the highly professional nature of that role. Decisions that teachers make in designing and executing instructional plans are far from trivial. These decisions depend on a sophisticated understanding of the content to be learned and the nature of learning itself. They require familiarity with the students and sophisticated judgments about the likely consequences of different courses of action.

At the same time, the professional nature of the role also imposes responsibilities on teachers. Working with a time-clock mentality prevents teachers as well as others from thinking of teaching as a profession. Professional educators must assume responsibility for understanding content, the cultural environments from which their students come, and the design of coherent instruction. Of course, textbooks and other materials can help, but teachers must make the critical decisions that affect student learning. Teaching is a profession—we must have no doubt about that. But if it is to be treated as a profession, then the responsibilities as well as the benefits deriving from that status must apply.

The framework for teaching rests on the assumption that teaching is indeed a profession and that the wise exercise of professional judgment distinguishes the exceptional teacher from the less accomplished. Such an orientation is integral to the framework and is evident in each of the components.

The framework for teaching is based on important assumptions:

- Derives from research.
- Reflects a new paradigm for learning and teaching that is grounded in the constructivist approach to teaching.
- Focuses on the purposeful nature of teaching.
- Creates a community of learners.
- Recognizes the role of appropriateness in making decisions.
- Asserts that teaching is a profession.

3 THE FOUR DOMAINS OF TEACHING RESPONSIBILITY

Although teachers sometimes feel pulled in many different directions—at one moment, a counselor; at another, a business manager—a unifying thread runs through the entire framework to provide an organizing structure. That thread consists of engaging students in learning important content. All the components of the framework serve this primary purpose. And in pursuit of important learning, a teacher creates, with the students, a community of learners, where all students feel respected and honored.

Each of the four domains of the framework refers to a distinct aspect of teaching. To some degree, the components within each domain form a coherent body of knowledge and skill, which can be the subject of focus independent of the other domains. Of course, there are many points of connection across domains. A teacher cannot demonstrate the highest level of skill in questioning and discussion techniques (Component 3b) if students do not feel the classroom environment is safe for taking risks and is one where their ideas will be respected (Component 2a). This chapter describes each domain, identifies common themes that run through the components, and explains the concepts underlying the four levels of performance that are displayed by teachers of different levels of skills.

Skills in Domain 1 are demonstrated primarily through the plans that teachers prepare to guide their teaching and ultimately through the success of those plans as implemented in the classroom. The plans may be included in a teacher's professional portfolio; the plan's effects must be observed through action in the classroom.

DOMAIN 1: PLANNING AND PREPARATION

The components in Domain 1 define how a teacher organizes the content that the students are to learn—how the teacher *designs* instruction (see Figure 3.1). All aspects of instructional planning are covered, beginning with a deep understanding of content and pedagogy and an understanding and appreciation of the students and what they bring to the educational encounter. But understanding the content is not sufficient. The content must be transformed through instructional design into sequences of activities and exercises that make it accessible to students. All elements of the instructional design—learning activities, materials, and strategies—should be appropriate to both the content and the students. In their content and process, assessment techniques must also reflect the instructional goals and should serve to document student progress during and at the end of a teaching episode.

Teachers who excel in Domain 1 design instruction that reflects an understanding of content and important concepts and principles within that content. Their design is coherent in its approach to topics, includes sound assessment methods, and is appropriate to the range of students in the class. The instructional design, *as a design,* works.

Figure 3.1

Components in Domain 1: Planning and Preparation

Component 1a:
Demonstrating Knowledge of Content and Pedagogy

Component 1b:
Demonstrating Knowledge of Students

Component 1c:
Selecting Instructional Goals

Component 1d:
Demonstrating Knowledge of Resources

Component 1e:
Designing Coherent Instruction

Component 1f:
Assessing Student Learning

DOMAIN 2: THE CLASSROOM ENVIRONMENT

Domain 2 consists of the interactions that occur in a classroom (see Figure 3.2). The interactions are themselves noninstructional, even though they are necessary for effective instruction. Such activities and tasks establish a comfortable and respectful classroom environment, which cultivates a culture for learning and creates a safe place for risk-taking. The atmosphere is businesslike, with noninstructional routines and procedures handled efficiently; student behavior is cooperative and nondisruptive; and the physical environment is supportive of the stated instructional purposes.

When students remember their teachers years later, it is often for the teacher's skill in Domain 2. Students recall the warmth and caring their favorite teachers demonstrated, the high expectations for achievement, and the teachers' commitment to their students. Students feel safe with these teachers and know that they can count on the teachers to be fair and, when necessary, compassionate.

Teachers who excel in Domain 2 consider their students as real people, with interests, concerns, and intellectual potential. In return, the students regard them as concerned and caring adults and entrust the teachers with their futures. Such teachers never forget their proper role as adults, so they don't try to be pals. They also know that their natural authority with students is grounded in their knowledge and expertise rather than in their role alone. These teachers are indisputably in charge, but their students regard them as a special sort of friend, a protector, a challenger, someone who will permit no harm. As such, these teachers are remembered for years with appreciation.

Skills in Domain 2 are demonstrated through classroom interaction and captured on paper through interviews with or surveys of students. These skills must be observed in action, either in person or on videotape.

Figure 3.2

Components in Domain 2: The Classroom Environment

Component 2a:
Creating an Environment of Respect and Rapport

Component 2b:
Establishing a Culture for Learning

Component 2c:
Managing Classroom Procedures

Component 2d:
Managing Student Behavior

Component 2e:
Organizing Physical Space

DOMAIN 3: INSTRUCTION

Domain 3 contains the components that are at the fundamental heart of teaching—the actual engagement of students in content. It is impossible to overstate the importance of Domain 3 (see Figure 3.3 on p. 32), which reflects the primary mission of schools: to enhance student learning. The components in Domain 3 are unified through the model of students constructing meaning and participating in a community of learners. Domain 3 components represent distinct elements of instruction.

Figure 3.3

Components in Domain 3: Instruction

Component 3a:
Communicating Clearly and Accurately

Component 3b:
Using Questioning and Discussion Techniques

Component 3c:
Engaging Students in Learning

Component 3d:
Providing Feedback to Students

Component 3e:
Demonstrating Flexibility and Responsiveness

Teachers who excel in Domain 3 create an atmosphere of excitement about the importance of learning and the significance of the content. They care deeply about their subject and invite students to share the journey of learning about it. Students are engaged in meaningful work, which carries significance beyond the next test and which can provide skills and knowledge necessary for answering important questions or contributing to important projects. Such teachers don't have to motivate their students because the ways in which teachers organize and present the content, the roles they encourage students to assume, and the student initiative they expect serve to motivate students to excel. The work is real and significant, and it is important to students as well as to teachers.

Skills in Domain 3 are demonstrated through classroom interaction, either observing in person or on videotape.

DOMAIN 4: PROFESSIONAL RESPONSIBILITIES

The components in Domain 4 are associated with being a true professional educator: they encompass the roles assumed outside of and in addition to those in the classroom with students (see Figure 3.4 on p. 33). Students rarely observe these activities; parents and the larger community observe them intermittently. But the activities are critical to preserving and enhancing the profession. Educators practice them primarily after their first few years of teaching, after they have mastered, to some degree, the details of classroom management and instruction.

Domain 4 consists of a wide range of professional responsibilities, from self-reflection and professional growth, to contributions made to the school and district, to contributions made to the profession as a whole. The components also include interactions with the families of students, contacts with the larger community, the maintenance of records and other paperwork, and advocacy for students.

Teachers who excel in Domain 4 are highly regarded by colleagues and parents. They can be depended on to serve students' interests and the larger community, and they are active in their professional organizations, in the school, and in the district. They are known as educators who go beyond the technical requirements of their jobs and contribute to the general well-being of the institutions of which they are a part.

Figure 3.4

Components in Domain 4:
Professional Responsibilities

Component 4a:
Reflecting on Teaching

Component 4b:
Maintaining Accurate Records

Component 4c:
Communicating with Families

Component 4d:
Contributing to the School and District

Component 4e:
Growing and Developing Professionally

Component 4f:
Showing Professionalism

Skills in Domain 4 are demonstrated through teacher interactions with colleagues, families, other professionals, and the larger community. Some of these interactions may be documented in logs and placed in a portfolio. It is the interactions themselves, however, that must be observed to indicate a teacher's skill and commitment.

COMMON THEMES

A number of themes apply to most of the components of the framework and are reflected in the entire instructional cycle, from planning and preparation through evaluation and reflection. They are described here, and their connection to the different domains and components explained.

EQUITY

Implicit in the entire framework, particularly those domains relating to interaction with students (Domains 2 and 3), is a commitment to equity. In an environment of respect and rapport, *all* students feel valued. When students are engaged in a discussion of a concept, *all* students are invited and encouraged to participate. When feedback is provided to students on their learning, it is provided to *all* students.

This equity imperative is particularly meaningful in the context of our history of elitism. Schools in the United States have traditionally served many students well. Students have been offered academic courses of high quality and have graduated to pursue opportunities in higher education. But our public schools have not served all students equally well. Those who have been underserved are primarily students of color, particularly in urban areas, and females, particularly in science and mathematics. And even when the inequities have not been institutionalized, as they were in segregated schools prior to 1954, they have been nearly as insidious.

A commitment to excellence is not complete without a commitment to equity. Such a commitment provides (1) equal opportunities for stimulating academic achievement, with the open doors to higher education and careers that result from success in that arena, and (2) additional levels of support for those traditionally underserved to enable them to overcome individual and communitywide doubts about their capability to succeed with distinction. In a school committed to equity, one would never hear a science or a physical education teacher in the faculty lounge say, "She did pretty well, *for a girl.*"

CULTURAL SENSITIVITY

Students may arrive at school with traditions that are different from or antagonistic to those of many U.S. classrooms. Children in some cultures, for instance, are taught not to look adults in the eye because it is a sign of disrespect; yet many U.S. teachers interpret a child's looking away as insolence. Similarly, the way questions are used in many classes is foreign to some students. When teachers use questions that they know the answer to as a way of checking, for example, whether students have done the assigned reading, these students are baffled: "Why would a teacher ask a question to which he already knows the answer? Clearly, this is not a real question; but if it is not a question, what is it?" Such thoughts interfere with a student's ability to participate fully, and the teacher may well conclude that the student is a slow learner. Other examples abound in research literature (Villegas 1991).

Teachers who are sensitive to the cultures of their students pay particular attention to Component 1b (demonstrating knowledge of students). In learning about students' backgrounds, these teachers ensure that they are aware of relevant information about cultural traditions, religious practices, and patterns of interaction that may affect a student's classroom participation. In addition, the teachers ensure that the materials they use (Components 1e and 3c) and the examples they employ (Component 3a) do not refer to items or traditions unfamiliar to students, or that they explain them fully. And they take particular care that in their communication with families (Component 4c) they demonstrate cultural respect.

HIGH EXPECTATIONS

Related to equity but distinct from it is a focus on high expectations. Accomplished professionals believe that all students are capable of extremely high standards of learning, and they organize their teaching accordingly. They are also aware of how expectations work. When teachers believe that some students are particularly capable or slow in learning, such expectations tend to become self-fulfilling prophecies.

The framework for professional practice reflects high expectations in a number of areas:

- Instructional goals (Component 1c).
- Levels of accomplishment established in a culture for learning (Component 2b).
- Questions posed in class (Component 3b).
- Feedback students receive (Component 3d).

• Communication with families about their children's work (Component 4c).

High expectations are necessarily grounded in clear and open standards for achievement. The characteristics of a good persuasive essay, for example, are rigorous, known to all students, and apply to all. And, echoing the commitment to equity, teachers are committed to helping all students reach the standard.

Based on their unique characteristics, some students may require additional time or support to reach a standard. They may be learning disabled, or they may learn very slowly. In these cases, high expectations will be based on the students' own unique history and reflect significant achievement *for them.*

DEVELOPMENTAL APPROPRIATENESS

How students engage with academic content is shaped in part by their level of intellectual development. Teachers can observe important patterns of development despite students' many individual differences. These patterns are especially important in certain academic areas—science and mathematics at all levels and literature and the social sciences at the high school level. For example, until students can conserve number, which is usually achieved by the time they are 6 or 7, they cannot understand addition facts. Similarly, until students understand the concept of separating and controlling variables, usually by age 11, they cannot design a scientific experiment independently. And until students can achieve formal thought (at about age 14), they will have trouble understanding the role of chance in history or engaging in serious literary criticism.

Attention to developmental appropriateness relates to many components, particularly (though not exclusively) those in Domain 1 (planning and preparation). Teachers who are sensitive to developmental patterns choose their instructional goals (Component 1c), activities and materials (Components 1e and 3c), and assessment strategies (Component 1f) carefully. But attention to child development also influences the other domains. Teachers demonstrate respect in developmentally appropriate ways (Component 2a). They ask developmentally appropriate questions (Component 3b) and provide feedback (Component 3d) in ways that stretch but do not overwhelm students intellectually.

ACCOMMODATING STUDENTS WITH SPECIAL NEEDS

An awareness of developmental appropriateness can be extended to include a sensitivity to students with special needs. Some of these needs are intellectual; others are physical or emotional. And in these days of greater inclusion of students with disabilities in regular classrooms, all teachers require at least some understanding of special needs.

Differing intellectual needs affect teachers' skill in many of the same areas of the framework that require sensitivity to developmental issues: attention to instructional goals, instructional design, and classroom interaction. Teachers who have students with physical limitations must also attend to the implications of how physical space is organized (Component 2e). Visually or hearing-impaired students must be situated in a classroom so they can see and hear to the maximum extent possible. Students with emotional needs impose particular responsibilities on teachers as they respond to student behavior (Component 2d), as well as to other aspects of student interaction in Domain 2 (the classroom environment) and Domain 3 (instruction).

APPROPRIATE USE OF TECHNOLOGY

Calculators, computers, CD-ROMs, video players, cameras, and other tools of technology are, to varying degrees, available in U.S. schools and classrooms. Using these tools to enhance learning is an important responsibility of today's teachers. Such tools can be used in classrooms with students (Components 3a and 3c) or as an aid to records management (Component 4b).

We need to remember that technological tools are just that—tools. They should never be considered ends in themselves, and they should not be misused. For example, if students learn to perform operations by using a calculator exclusively, they may not know how to do the problem without it. That is, if students don't understand the *concept* of multiplication or how multiplying by 10 affects a product, then using a calculator to get the right answer leaves them vulnerable. Once students have acquired the relevant concepts, however, the calculator can save a great deal of time.

Teachers and schools must also be aware that the private resources available to students in the area of technology are extremely uneven. Many families now have computers at home, complete with games and CD-ROM players. Many others do not. The familiarity with technology enjoyed by the children from those different families is correspondingly diverse and is reflected in how they can use technological tools in their academic work. Part of a school's responsibility is to provide access to the technological world for all students.

LEVELS OF PERFORMANCE

Each element of a component has four levels of performance: unsatisfactory, basic, proficient, and distinguished. The levels range from describing teachers who are still striving to master the rudiments of teaching (unsatisfactory) to highly accomplished professionals who are able to share their expertise (distinguished).

The levels of performance are especially useful if the components are used for supervision and evaluation. But even when they are employed to help with self-assessment or to support mentoring or coaching relationships, they can inform a professional discussion and suggest areas for further growth.

UNSATISFACTORY

The teacher does not yet appear to understand the concepts underlying the component. Working on the fundamental practices associated with the elements will enable the teacher to grow and develop in this area.

BASIC

The teacher appears to understand the concepts underlying the component and attempts to implement its elements. But implementation is sporadic, intermittent, or otherwise not entirely successful. Additional reading, discussion, visiting classrooms of other teachers, and experience (particularly supported by a mentor) will enable the teacher to become proficient in this area.

For supervision or evaluation, this level is minimally competent—improvement is likely with experience, and little or no actual harm is done to students.

PROFICIENT

The teacher clearly understands the concepts underlying the component and implements it well. Most experienced, capable teachers will regard themselves and be regarded by others as performing at this level.

DISTINGUISHED

Teachers at this level are master teachers and make a contribution to the field, both in and outside their school. Their classrooms operate at a qualitatively different level, consisting of a community of learners, with students highly motivated and engaged and assuming considerable responsibility for their own learning.

4
CREATING A
PROFESSIONAL PORTFOLIO

Creating a professional portfolio can benefit a teacher in many of the same ways that teachers have observed portfolios benefitting students. For example, when students select for a portfolio their best work of writing or mathematics problem solving, they must ask themselves, "What makes a piece of writing good?" or "Why is this problem-solving approach better than this other one?" Similarly, teachers who are asked to submit a portfolio when applying for national board certification have discovered the power derived from selecting and commenting on their best teaching.

In deciding what to include in a portfolio, teachers must reflect on their best work and determine what represents that work. A portfolio can become, then, a manifestation of a teacher's professional philosophy, showing written and perhaps video work. A portfolio assembled in the context of the framework for professional practice can achieve more than one put together without such a framework. An agreed-upon definition of good teaching offers a structure for a portfolio's contents. A teacher can use a portfolio to document attainment of the components of the framework and to stimulate professional conversation.

PURPOSES

A teacher's portfolio can serve many different purposes, depending on how (or if) the framework is used throughout a school or district.

FOR SELF-REFLECTION AND ANALYSIS

Assembling items for a portfolio is a powerful vehicle for professional reflection and analysis. When a teacher decides to include one instructional unit over another or the video of a certain class instead of another, that judgment requires determining how the features of one unit are superior to others. "What makes it good?" "How could it have been strengthened even further?" These thought processes, particularly if accompanied by discussion, enable a teacher to enhance instructional decisions. And such enhancement is precisely the value of reflection and analysis.

TO SUPPORT MENTORING AND COACHING RELATIONSHIPS

When an experienced teacher visits the classroom of a novice teacher or another veteran and the two discuss the lesson afterwards, both usually benefit. But the discussion is, of necessity, limited by what occurred in the class, supplemented by oral background and explanation that the host teacher provides.

A collection of artifacts can extend the scope of these discussions and illuminate the positions both teachers take. For example, suppose a mentor observes that the development of a concept within a lesson lacked coherence and that students left the class without a clear understanding of the concept. The novice might use a complete unit plan to describe how the concept is meant to develop over the course of several lessons and explain the coherence of the larger sequence of activities. Even if the observed lesson could be improved still more with a tighter structure, the unit plan enables both teachers to see the observed lesson within an overall context. Similarly, suppose a mentor comments on a student's behavior—the student is not paying attention or is disruptive. The novice can provide context for the student's behavior by referring to a log of family contact, which illustrates the number and type of conversations that the teacher has had with the student's family.

A portfolio is not a substitute for classroom observation and professional discussion, which compose the heart of a mentoring or coaching relationship. Rather, it is an extension and enhancement of that discussion to cover *all* aspects of teaching, not merely those observed in a single class.

TO STRENGTHEN A RESUMÉ

When a teacher wants to move to a professionally more rewarding or more challenging position, the teacher must document excellence. Whether the goal is a teaching position in another school or district or a leadership position within the same district (e.g., lead teacher, team leader, or mentor), supporting the application with evidence of work with students and colleagues is helpful. Particularly when the position is in a different school or district where the teacher's work is not well known, a portfolio can supplement the interview process. Indeed, educators recognize that most interviews are inadequate to communicate the full range of a teacher's craft. In an interview, it is difficult to provide evidence of skill in planning; interaction with students; feedback to students; and contributions to the school, district, and profession. But print and video entries in a well-planned portfolio can show it clearly and dramatically.

CONTENTS

A teaching portfolio contains any items that an educator selects to put in it. Clearly, the contents of a novice teacher's portfolio are somewhat different from those of an experienced veteran. Purpose is critical to what goes into a portfolio. For example, when a teacher collects samples of student writing over the course of a year or more, the teacher is looking for and helping the student to see progress over time. In contrast, when an art student selects pieces of art to submit for the Advanced Placement (AP) Studio Art portfolio, the works are those that both satisfy the requirements of AP and illustrate the student's best efforts.

The same considerations apply to a professional portfolio. If a beginning teacher wants to demonstrate improved skills in instructional planning, he may include in his portfolio a lesson or unit plan from October and another from December; these support the teacher's

discussions of progress with a mentor. Or, if a teacher is planning to apply for a position as a team leader or mentor, her portfolio may contain a single unit plan; a videotape illustrating her skill in establishing a productive classroom environment and engaging students in a topic; and logs to demonstrate her contributions to the school, interaction with families, and reflection on teaching.

The portfolio contents recommended in this book are naturally those that document the framework for professional practice. Other entries are certainly possible and can further strengthen the presentation of a teacher's professional skills. But the entries recommended here are discussed in terms of how they illuminate a teacher's skill in relation to the framework.

A THREE-WEEK UNIT PLAN

By completing a three-week unit plan, a teacher demonstrates the thinking that has resulted in how he treats a topic with a group of students. The unit plan suggested here is brief, consisting of a single page (see Figure 4.1 on p. 41). The boxes for each day are used to note the topic for the day and generally how students will engage with that topic.

Of course, units vary in length. Teachers can adapt the form to accommodate longer units by using more than one form, or to accommodate shorter units by using only a portion of the form. The unit plan illustrates a teacher's skill in Component 1e: designing coherent instruction.

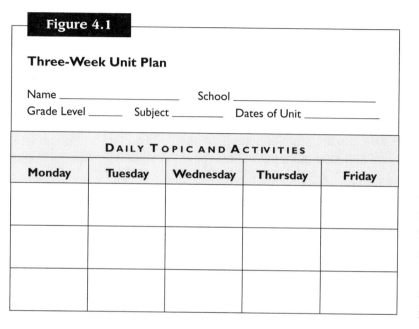

Figure 4.1

Three-Week Unit Plan

Name _____ School _____

Grade Level _____ Subject _____ Dates of Unit _____

DAILY TOPIC AND ACTIVITIES				
Monday	**Tuesday**	**Wednesday**	**Thursday**	**Friday**

INSTRUCTION PLAN FOR A SINGLE LESSON

A teacher provides detailed information about the content and procedures for a single lesson in the Instruction Plan for a Single Lesson (see Figure 4.2 on p. 42). The questions focus on different aspects of planning: information about the students, instructional goals, activities students will do, materials, and assessment methods. The instruction plan provides information about the different components of Domain 1.

SAMPLES OF ASSESSMENT PROCEDURES

The instruction plan includes questions (Questions 9 and 10) about assessing student learning (Component 1f). Question 9 also asks that a teacher attach any assessment materials used with students. Including these materials in a portfolio provides information on a teacher's approach to assessment in a manner not available from any other source.

Sample assessment procedures are most meaningful when the instructional goals to which they are aligned are identified. Such information enables a reader of the portfolio to understand the teacher's intent in using different assessment methodologies and the aspects of student performance that the teacher particularly valued.

Some student work that is part of an assessment, such as an essay or a lab report, is evaluated on the basis of the teacher's judgment. In such cases, the scoring rubric that the teacher uses to evaluate that work should also be included in the portfolio.

KNOWLEDGE OF STUDENTS AND RESOURCES

The Knowledge of Students and Resources Sheet (see Figure 4.3 on p. 43) provides an indication of a teacher's expertise in Component 1b (demonstrating knowledge of students) and Component 1d (demonstrating knowledge of resources). Answering the questions helps teachers reflect on and demonstrate their skill in learning about both their students and the resources available for their work.

All teachers should try to accommodate students' background knowledge and skills as this information relates to the content, students' interests outside school, and their cultural heritage. What

Figure 4.2

Instruction Plan for a Single Lesson

Name _____ School _____

Grade Level _____ Subject _____ Date _____

1. Briefly describe the students in this class, including those with special needs. *(Component 1b)*

2. What are your goals for the lesson? What do you want the students to learn? *(Component 1c)*

3. Why are these goals suitable for this group of students? *(Component 1c)*

4. How do these goals support the district's curriculum, state frameworks, and content standards? *(Components 1a and 1c)*

5. How do these goals relate to broader curriculum goals in the discipline as a whole or in other disciplines? *(Component 1c)*

6. How do you plan to engage students in the content? What will you do? What will the students do? (Include time estimates.) *(Component 1e)*

7. What difficulties do students typically experience in this area, and how do you plan to anticipate these difficulties? *(Component 1a)*

8. What instructional materials or other resources, if any, will you use? *(Component 1d)*

9. How do you plan to assess student achievement of the goals? What procedures will you use? (Attach any tests or performance tasks, with accompanying scoring guides or rubrics.) *(Component 1f)*

10. How do you plan to make use of the results of the assessment? *(Component 1f)*

students bring to the instructional event from these areas affects their experience with the material and the activities.

The form includes questions about a teacher's knowledge of resources that help in teaching, as well as resources that are available for students who need them independently of a particular instructional setting. Both are important; a school may have personnel to assist with the latter, such as offering special education services or coordinating with social service agencies.

Context is critical in establishing expectations about a teacher's knowledge of students. For example, an instrumental music teacher or a physical education teacher interacts with hundreds of students. Consequently, such a teacher is only able to have the most general knowledge of students' interests and skills. Similarly, the degree and kind of knowledge of individual students is different for a kindergarten teacher than it is for a high school English teacher. What teachers can expect of themselves in the different contexts varies accordingly.

VIDEOTAPE OF A CLASS

A videotape reveals a teacher's skill in the components that depend on interaction with students, and it can serve as a substitute for live observation. An observer (such as a mentor) can witness how a teacher demonstrates all the standards in Domains 2 and 3. For example, the mentor can see the specific techniques a teacher uses to establish an environment of respect and rapport (Component 2a) and a culture for learning (Component 2b) or to conduct a class discussion (Component 3b). A mentor can use the Classroom Observation Record (see Figure 4.4 on p. 44) to record information and write specific (but brief) instances of the different components.

Figure 4.3

Knowledge of Students and Resources Sheet

Name _____   School _____
Grade Level _____   Subject _____   School Year _____

1. What techniques do you use to learn about your students'
   . . . background knowledge and skills?

   . . . interests outside school?

   . . . cultural heritage?

2. What resources are available to enhance your students' experience in this subject? (Examples are films, videos, museums, and experts in the community.)

3. What resources are available for students if needed? (Examples are counseling, medical facilities, and clothing contributions.)

Figure 4.4

Classroom Observation Record

Name _____ School _____

Grade Level _____ Subject _____ School Year _____

Observer Name _____ Position _____

Component 2a: *Creating an Environment of Respect and Rapport*	Component 3a: *Communicating Clearly and Accurately*
Component 2b: *Establishing a Culture for Learning*	Component 3b: Using Questioning and Discussion Techniques
Component 2c: *Managing Classroom Procedures*	Component 3c: *Engaging Students in Learning*
Component 2d: *Managing Student Behavior*	Component 3d: *Providing Feedback to Students*
Component 2e: *Organizing Physical Space*	Component 3e: *Demonstrating Flexibility and Responsiveness*

Of course, not all elements of all components will be demonstrated in a single tape segment. Within a 15–20 minute section of a lesson, for example, a teacher may not exhibit flexibility and responsiveness (Component 3e) because the need may not arise. Most elements of the components in Domains 2 and 3, however, can be demonstrated in a videotape the same as they would be in an observed lesson. But unlike a classroom observation, the videotape can become a physical part of a portfolio, a record of practice until replaced.

Creating a videotape presents technical challenges that should be kept in mind so that the tape is of the highest possible quality. For example, student voices are frequently difficult to hear, and the camera should not, if possible, be pointed toward the windows. Also, if the camera is focused entirely on the teacher, student reactions to questions, discussion, and activities cannot be observed.

A videotape produced to put in a professional portfolio to support conversations with a mentor or coach or to strengthen a resumé does not require the technical sophistication of a tape presented, for example, for national board certification or for state licensing. Technical considerations are not as important for such informal use. The mentor, after all, knows the teacher, can visit the class in person, and can engage the teacher in conversation. For national board certification, on the other hand, a videotape is evaluated by assessors who have never met the candidate and probably never will. Therefore, the tape must speak for itself.

Educators need to remember that watching a videotape is an imperfect substitute for observing an actual class. On the one hand, watching a videotape is easier: Because an observer can see only what the camera captures, the observer's attention can focus entirely on what is in the direct eye of the camera. On the other hand, the observer misses much of what is important in a classroom. For example, a student may ask a question to which the teacher responds. Unless the camera then returns to the student, an observer never knows the student's reaction to the response. And depending on where the camera is pointed, an observer may not know how the rest of the class reacted to the exchange. Such things are rarely in doubt during an actual observation; an observer's eyes constantly survey the entire scene, picking up the relevant information to support an impression.

A classroom "climate" doesn't always translate onto a videotape. Teachers and students establish ways of interacting that are either "warm" or "cold," respectful or disrespectful. A classroom may or may not be a safe environment in which to take intellectual risks. Indications of such diverse classrooms are often small and easily missed in a videotape, particularly if it focuses entirely on the teacher. Student interaction helps tremendously in determining what is important about a classroom's environment.

Even with these technical challenges and limitations, a videotape of a class is an enormously powerful addition to a teacher's portfolio. It demonstrates in ways that no pieces of paper can a teacher's skill in the central task of teaching, namely, interacting with students and engaging them in important content.

INSTRUCTIONAL ARTIFACTS OF IN-CLASS ASSIGNMENTS AND HOMEWORK

A sample of instructional practice in the form of an in-class or homework assignment can provide a window on classroom life. As part of a portfolio, it demonstrates a teacher's skill in engaging students in learning (Component 3c). Such a sample may include the following elements:

• Name of the topic or concept to be developed (e.g., prime numbers in mathematics or setting in literature).

• Teacher's intent in giving the assignment: What does the teacher hope students will learn as a result of completing the assignment (i.e., the instructional goals)?

• Directions to students on what they are to do with respect to the topic (e.g., perform an investigation with prime numbers or explain the role of setting in a novel).

• Actual material that students use (e.g., a worksheet or lab form).

• Samples of student work.

• A commentary describing the value of the assignment in promoting student learning.

Of course, in actual daily use, an in-class assignment may be given orally, whereas it must be in written form for a portfolio. The writing does not need to be elaborate; a teacher can simply jot down the instructions given to students while making an assignment or getting them started on an activity to put in a portfolio.

If a teacher asks students to use instructional materials for the assignment in the portfolio, copies of these should be included in the portfolio. For example, if students are completing a data table for a science investigation, a copy of the format should be included. If the assignment is to complete a worksheet, a copy of the worksheet should be attached.

SAMPLES OF STUDENT WORK

Providing samples of student work in a portfolio demonstrates the extent of student engagement in a task (Component 3c) and may possibly provide evidence of student pride in their work (an element in Component 2b). The samples may be photocopies of the students' work or other records rather than the actual work, which will probably have been returned to students. If a teacher's feedback is also included, these samples demonstrate the teacher's skill in Component 3d (providing feedback to students).

Student work gains meaning if a reader understands the context that produced it. Therefore, if possible, student work should either be for the assignment included in the portfolio as an instructional artifact or for an assignment shown on a videotape.

A portfolio can quickly become too large to handle if all the work from a class is included. Three or four samples representing the full range of student responses are sufficient to demonstrate the instructional challenge a teacher faced and reveal the range of success different students attained in engaging productively with the content.

Samples of student work should be accompanied by a brief commentary explaining what each sample reveals about a student's level of understanding and progress in the subject, and the next steps indicated. These comments and analysis provide rich material for discussion among colleagues. The Instructional Artifact Sheet (see Figure 4.5 on p. 47) guides teachers in selecting materials to include with an instructional artifact.

Figure 4.5

Instructional Artifact Sheet

Name _____ School _____

Grade Level _____ Subject _____ Date _____

Concept or Topic _____

Instructional Goal or Goals_____

1. Attach directions or an assignment that engages students in learning about the concept or topic cited above. Examples are a worksheet, homework or class assignment, project guidelines, or a problem.

2. Provide several samples of student work on this assignment. They should reflect the full range of student ability in your class and include feedback you provided to the students on their papers.

3. Write a brief commentary about the assignment, answering the following questions:

• What is the context of the assignment in terms of students' prior knowledge and the other topics they have been studying?

• What do the samples of student work tell you about the students' level of understanding?

• How does the assignment help students develop their understanding?

• What do you plan to do next with these students?

REFLECTION SHEET

The Reflection Sheet, as its name suggests, provides an opportunity for teachers to reflect on a particular lesson to determine if their instructional goals were met and how they might teach the same topic or concept another time (see Figure 4.6 on p. 48). Many teachers engage in this type of activity on an on-going but informal basis as they consider the effectiveness of their instructional decisions. The form simply provides a format for conscious self-evaluation by the teacher and offers specific examples of how Component 4a (reflecting on teaching) has been attained.

The Reflection Sheet is most effective in a portfolio when it is used in conjunction with either a videotape or an instructional artifact, because these provide a context for the reflection. Of course, the sheet can also be used in conjunction with a lesson that a mentor, coach, or supervisor observes to provide the teacher's own interpretation of class events.

Figure 4.6

Reflection Sheet

Name _____ School _____

Grade Level _____ Subject _____ Date _____

1. As I reflect on the lesson, to what extent were students productively engaged? *(Component 4a)*

2. Did the students learn what I intended? Were my instructional goals met? How do I know, or how and when will I know? *(Components 1f and 4a)*

3. Did I alter my goals or instructional plan as I taught the lesson? Why? *(Components 1e and 3e)*

4. If I had the opportunity to teach this lesson again to this same group of students, what would I do differently? Why? *(Component 4a)*

LOGS:
FAMILY CONTACT
PARTICIPATION IN SCHOOL
AND DISTRICT PROJECTS
PROFESSIONAL CONTRIBUTIONS
PROFESSIONAL DEVELOPMENT

Logs of professional activities may provide the only documentation of a teacher's contact with families (Figure 4.7), contribution to the school and district (Figure 4.8), professional contributions (Figure 4.9), and professional development activities (Figure 4.10). (See p. 49 for figures.) Often, teachers undertake such efforts as part of their responsibilities, but they frequently have little record of what they have done. Teachers find that maintaining logs enables them to demonstrate the breadth of their responsibilities. As part of a portfolio, the logs provide evidence of a teacher's commitment to these aspects of teaching and illustrate the diverse ways in which Component 4c (communicating with families), Component 4d (contributing to the school and district), Component 4e (growing and developing professionally), and Component 4f (showing professionalism) are manifested.

Figure 4.7

Family Contact Log

Name _____ School _____ School Year _____

Date	Person Contacted	Type of Contact (person, phone)	Purpose	Outcome

Figure 4.9

Professional Contribution Log

Name _____ School _____ School Year _____

Date	Event or Service (e.g., conference presentation, mentoring)	Contribution

Figure 4.8

School and District Contribution Log

Name _____ School _____ School Year _____

Date	Event (e.g., committee meeting, open house)	Contribution

Figure 4.10

Professional Development Log

Name _____ School _____ School Year _____

Date	Event (e.g., workshop, conference, course)	Benefits Derived

RESEARCH LOG

For many teachers, questions abound about such issues as the effectiveness of different instructional approaches, different ways of sequencing particular learning activities, and the use of one set of materials over another. Unfortunately, most educators, because they are confronted with extremely demanding jobs, do not find the time to ask these questions systematically and to develop a plan for answering them.

The Research Log provides a vehicle for structuring a teacher's approach to asking such questions and seeking answers (see Figure 4.11). It invites teachers to frame questions carefully, determine the information needed to answer the questions, and prepare plans to collect that information. Teachers then have the opportunity to summarize and draw conclusions from their findings. The results of such research are, of course, of great interest to other educators and will find a ready audience through professional conferences and publications. In conducting classroom research, teachers demonstrate the highest level of Component 4e: growing and developing professionally.

Figure 4.11

Research Log

Name _____ School _____

Grade Level _____ Subject _____ School Year_____

1. Write a question that you would like to answer about student learning or your teaching.

2. What information do you need to answer the question?

3. In the Action Plan, indicate how you plan to answer the question.

Action Plan

Step	Actions	Time Line
1		
2		
3		
4		

4. Summary and Conclusions: If you are able to complete the research, answer the following questions on separate paper:

- What have you learned from this project?

- What additional questions do you have?

- Do you plan to alter your practice as a result of this project? If so, how?

5 Using the Framework

This book presents a framework for teaching. Whether it is beneficial to educators depends on how it is used, because, like any tool, it can be misused. This chapter provides guidance on how to become familiar with and use the framework.

Understanding the Framework

Before teachers or schools can use the framework for teaching, the people who will be working with it should spend time understanding the components and determining their applicability to different situations.

Appearance in Different Contexts

As described in Chapter 2, the components are generic; that is, they are designed to apply to any teaching situation. Their actual manifestations, however, differ in various contexts. Although teachers work to develop a culture for learning in their classrooms (Component 2b), the specific actions taken by a 2nd grade teacher, a middle school science teacher, and a high school Spanish teacher are quite different. By understanding how the different components are manifested in different contexts, educators can best appreciate the construct underlying the specific behavior and therefore the real meaning of each component. Educators need to translate the components and their elements into specific, observable examples in different contexts.

APPLICABILITY AND WEIGHTING

If the framework is used for supervision or evaluation of teaching, the applicability and weighting of each component must be examined. Do all the components apply to every teaching situation, or are there some that do not? For instance, do high school band teachers establish and maintain contact with families of their students (Component 4c)? Such contact is different, no doubt, from that of a primary teacher. But most educators agree that high school band teachers do maintain contact in their own way.

Similarly, do all the *elements* of all the components apply to every situation? For example, one element of Component 2c (managing classroom procedures) concerns the supervision of volunteers and paraprofessionals. Clearly, if a teacher has such resources available, managing them is an important element of classroom management. But if such assistance is not available (and it is not in a majority of classrooms), then this element does not apply.

Weighting is a related concern. Are all the components equally important, or are some more important than others? Are some more important in some settings? Educators may argue, for example, that in a special education setting, the Domain 2 components (the classroom environment) are more important than the Domain 3 components (instruction). Grounds for such weighting are based on the belief that for special education students, the classroom environment is critical to their general attitude toward school. Consequently, their academic success depends on their feeling safe and comfortable in a classroom.

Others may argue that a teacher's knowledge of content and pedagogy (Component 1a) is central to the teacher's success with students. Or, they may argue that such knowledge, when combined with skill in questioning and discussion techniques (Component 3b), is critical to teachers of advanced academic content. The people involved must make these decisions, which may be different in different settings.

When the framework is used for self-assessment and reflection, mentoring, and peer coaching, decisions about weighting are unnecessary. Instead, the components simply provide the basis for feedback and guidance for professional development.

DETERMINING MANIFESTATION, APPLICABILITY, AND WEIGHTING

To understand the different appearance of the components, their applicability, and their relative weight in various contexts, educators should carefully consider each component. This effort is best done through a series of group meetings, focused on readings, videotapes, and structured discussion. A group can use the following steps as a guide for understanding a component:

• Each member reads the "Rationale and Explanation" section of the component and considers its elements and descriptions of levels of performance (Chapter 6 provides this information for each component).

• As time and resources allow, group members read different research articles related to the component and prepare a summary for the group.

• Members interpret the component and the elements for their own settings, describing what specific actions or statements they would expect to see or hear from a teacher who is applying the component at different levels of performance. These descriptions may be written on newsprint and displayed (so they can be easily referred to) or simply discussed.

• For those components that are visible in the classroom, group members watch a videotape of a lesson, citing specific actions or oral exchanges that illustrate elements of the component. Of course, a single videotape may illustrate many components. The group may wish to view the videotape after it has considered all the components in, for example, an entire domain.

• Group members share their perspectives and interpretations of the components, isolating important differences and achieving a consensus on the components' operational meaning. The group may also determine how the appearance of the different components varies from one context to another.

• The group determines the relative importance of the components and elements in different settings. Some may not apply at all; others may be critically important.

These discussions do not happen quickly, nor can they be rushed. Indeed, for many educators, such conversations are at the heart of the value derived from using the framework. By focusing on different components of practice and by translating them into individual contexts, teachers, curriculum specialists, and administrators all come to a common understanding and common definitions of what constitutes excellent teaching and how it manifests itself in the classroom, school, and district. The framework, then, while central to this activity, is merely a vehicle for rich conversation that yields such consensus.

USING THE FRAMEWORK FOR REFLECTION AND SELF-ASSESSMENT

The most powerful use of the framework, and one which should accompany any other use, is for reflection and self-assessment. Research has clearly demonstrated that the effects of reflection improve teaching. Using a framework to guide such reflection enhances the value of the activity and makes teaching more purposeful, thoughtful, and rewarding.

Reflection and self-assessment are individual activities, conducted in the privacy of a teacher's own classroom and thoughts. Although the results of reflection and self-assessment may play a part in other shared activities—such as mentoring or peer coaching—reflection and self-assessment are conducted individually.

Reflection is most informative if accompanied by making a videotape of a teacher's own teaching. Teachers may experience a natural reluctance to view themselves on video. The first time is frequently a shock, since we tend not to imagine ourselves as others see us. Making a tape requires courage as well as curiosity. But once a teacher gets over the initial hesitation, the benefits are enormous. There is simply no other way to understand the details of how one's lessons are presented and received by students.

Technical and practical difficulties need to be considered. Some schools have videotaping equipment easily available; in others, it must be scheduled in advance. Technical issues (described in Chapter 4) should be considered. But with experience, both the practical difficulties and the psychological hesitation will decrease, and teachers will find that they derive great benefit from observing their own classroom on videotape.

To use the framework for reflection and self-assessment, the following steps are recommended:

• Carefully read the explanations and rationales, the elements, and the levels of performance for each component (see Chapter 6).

• Determine if any component or elements do not apply to your situation.

• Collect information on your teaching. This material can include what you might put in a teaching portfolio (see Chapter 4): Three-Week Unit Plan; Instruction Plan for a Single Lesson; Knowledge of Students and Resources Sheet; Instructional Artifact Sheet; Reflection Sheet; samples of student work; logs of professional development activities, contacts with families, and contributions to the school and district; and at least one videotape of yourself teaching.

• For the components and elements that apply, and most of them will, determine how you exhibit the components. For example, how do you learn about your students' knowledge, skills, and backgrounds (Component 1b)? How do you communicate clearly with your students (Component 3a)? Note specific ways in which you do each of these.

• For those components that are seen primarily in your interaction with students in a classroom (Domains 2 and 3), view a videotape of yourself teaching a lesson, and identify specific actions, words, or interactions that provide an indication of your expertise for each component. You may also see patterns of interactions that will be illuminating.

• For those components that are demonstrated primarily outside the classroom (Domains 1 and 4), review the appropriate entries in your portfolio, and determine what specific indications you can provide to demonstrate your skill in each component.

• Carefully read the levels of performance for the elements of each component (see Chapter 6). Decide which level best describes your teaching for each element, citing examples from the videotape or other materials to support your decision. The levels you select will provide a profile of you as a teacher and may suggest areas in which you want to concentrate your energies for future professional growth.

Using the Framework for Mentoring and Induction

The complexity of teaching can be daunting for those new to the profession. Teaching is one of the few professions in which novices must assume the same responsibilities as veterans in the field. In some teaching environments, rookies are presented with the most challenging students, the largest number of preparations, inadequate or limited materials, and the least attractive rooms. First-year teachers are far more likely than veterans not to have their own room, working on an itinerant basis and moving their supplies from room to room on a cart.

All these conditions lead to stress for a novice teacher, which can lead to high rates of attrition. All schools and districts want to help new teachers be successful, but their first concern is to retain them in the profession. People who enter the field of education often have other options. If teaching is too difficult, too stressful, too unrewarding, or too highly politicized, they may take their talents into another arena.

The task for an induction program and for mentors in such a program is not to make teaching easy; that is probably impossible, given the realities of classroom life. Teaching is not an easy job, period. But it is rewarding—or at least it can be. The challenge, then, is for a mentor teacher to help a novice experience sufficient rewards in daily life to master the complex details needed to become truly accomplished. Once the thousands of small skills are mastered, the patterns established, the curriculum understood, and the procedures routinized, teachers are free to exercise their creativity. But in the beginning, accomplishing these activities can seem hopeless; there is far too much to do, and the students and their parents do not tolerate many false starts.

One of the greatest gifts an experienced teacher can offer the profession is to serve as a mentor to a novice. By sharing acquired wisdom, the veteran can spare the beginner hours of time and countless occasions of self-doubt. By serving as a friendly critic or just a patient listener, the mentor can assist the novice in identifying those areas of teaching that will benefit most from focused attention. The mentor can help by analyzing the novice's plans and classroom interactions and by making specific and substantive suggestions for improvement. In addition, the mentor can serve as a demonstration teacher, modeling techniques of effective instruction.

The framework for teaching plays an important role in the mentor-novice relationship. If the novice has conducted a self-assessment using the framework, this analysis is most helpful in determining which areas of teaching need primary attention. Alternatively, the mentor may observe the novice in action or review lesson and unit plans and make suggestions, using the framework to show areas needing attention. The components provide a road map to teaching; by using the road map, both the mentor and the beginning teacher can focus their energies on those areas of teaching where improvement will have the largest overall effect.

With beginning teachers, the first area that usually needs to be mastered is the classroom environment (Domain 2). Components in Domain 2 relate to aspects of the classroom that are not directly instructional, such as creating an environment of respect and rapport, developing a culture for learning, managing student behavior, and making physical arrangements. Probably most important for the novice, Domain 2 also includes managing procedures. Most educators find that they must have these procedural matters mastered before they can let their creative energies loose on the instructional aspects of teaching.

Another rich area for mentoring is content and, more specifically, content-related pedagogical expertise. A new teacher in high school history can learn much about the teaching of history from a mentor in the same department. A teacher with expertise in teaching elementary mathematics has much to offer a novice preparing a 3rd grade math lesson. Such expertise is valuable and should be made available whenever possible.

Novice teachers can also learn from a mentor whose expertise lies in a different content area or with students of a different level, particularly with respect to general pedagogical issues and the classroom environment (Domain 2). In general, a mentor doesn't need content expertise to notice that some students are dominating the discussion or that students are not engaged in the activities. A teacher's skill in questioning and discussion techniques is independent of the content being explored. Therefore, even though content expertise is valuable from a mentor, much assistance may be derived from a mentoring relationship with a teacher from a different specialty. In fact, such cross-fertilization can provide other benefits not available when the novice and the mentor share a similar background and teaching assignment. Mentors who work with novice teachers must cultivate the skills of providing feedback and suggestions constructively. These consultative skills enable a mentor to offer support that

may otherwise be perceived as criticism.

One technique involves making positive comments about a lesson or a unit plan. Sometimes, the tendency is to focus exclusively on the areas of performance that need improvement and omit references to the many strengths displayed. All teachers, particularly those new to the profession, need to hear their good points described and commented upon. They may not be sure that a particular approach is a good one, and hearing it praised by a respected teacher can go a long way toward building confidence. An effective mentor builds on the identified strengths of the novice and provides for training in areas needing refinement or growth.

When a mentor sees room for improvement, a wise approach is to focus on purposes and to ask questions before making suggestions. Most novices are eager to adopt better practices, but advice makes more sense when it is presented as a method to better achieve the novice teacher's purposes. Therefore, conversations about the teacher's intentions and ways to achieve the teacher's goals help a novice appreciate that all instructional decisions have consequences and that some accomplish the teacher's purposes better than others.

USING THE FRAMEWORK FOR PEER COACHING

Professional educators continually try to learn. They recognize that their education does not end when they receive their degrees, and they continue to incorporate research findings into their practice. They have internalized the idea that all good teaching can improve;

they seek out other outstanding teachers and both learn from and teach their colleagues. The peer coaching relationship is one of professional synergy, with each participant offering insights that result in the improvement of teaching. Teachers who engage in a peer coaching relationship acknowledge that good teaching can improve and that in a profession as demanding and as subject to new research findings as teaching, everyone's professional responsibility should involve enhancing one's skills.

The framework for teaching enhances the peer coaching relationship among educators. Time is well spent when peers conduct self-assessments and then discuss areas of perceived weakness and strength with each other. When teachers use the same framework, they improve communication because they're using the same set of concepts and terms to describe phenomena. In addition, by using the framework, they can be sure that the areas chosen for improvement are truly those most in need of work.

Colleagues can use the framework in many ways to enhance the peer coaching process. First, self-assessments show which areas need improvement. Then, in consultation with their colleagues, teachers can request assistance in those areas, asking their peers to review lesson and unit plans or to observe a lesson. The subsequent conversations are rich even if they are not based on the framework. When such dialogue is grounded in the language of the framework, however, it is enhanced by the shared understanding that derives from a common view of the teaching process.

Considerations that apply to the mentor-novice relationship also apply to the peer coaching partnership. For example, expertise in content as well as skills in providing substantive and supportive feedback benefits both individuals. But since the people involved in a peer coaching relationship are both experienced teachers, the dialogue reflects that parity. Experienced teachers recognize one another's strengths—how they offer and accept instructional suggestions is a mark of professionalism.

USING THE FRAMEWORK FOR SUPERVISION

Current supervision theory states that to be effective, supervisory practices must be regulated in large part by the teacher. The teacher decides what happens in a classroom, and instructional practice cannot improve without these decisions being the best possible. The framework can transform what is generally the rather meaningless ritual of supervisory evaluation into a powerful process for thinking about instructional excellence.

PROCEDURES

Typically, every school or district has procedures for supervision and evaluation. Sometimes, state law or a negotiated agreement dictates the procedures. They generally include provisions about the type of data to be used and time lines for different portions of the process. A certain number of classroom observations supported by conferences are usually required. Because, generally speaking, any set of criteria may be used as a framework for the supervisory process, the framework for teaching can fill that role.

GOAL SETTING

The supervisory process generally begins with goal setting. In the absence of an agreed-upon framework for teaching, these goals may or may not reflect a teacher's greatest need. A teacher who has engaged in self-assessment and reflection, based on the framework for teaching, has probably identified areas that can benefit from focused attention. Also, the supervisor, through either classroom observation or school interactions, may have identified specific components that can profit from further analysis. The teacher and the supervisor, then, as a result of preliminary thought and reflection, jointly determine the areas that will be the focus for the year's effort.

These goals may come from any part of the framework and, indeed, may include a number of different components. For less experienced teachers, the goals may be concentrated in Domain 2 (the classroom environment). Concentrating on the identified components ensures both the teacher and the supervisor that the greatest benefit to teaching will result from the supervisory efforts.

DATA COLLECTION

Initially, the selected goals for the teacher may be only preliminary, needing reassessment after more careful documentation. Suppose a teacher and supervisor determine that they want to work on Component 3c: engaging students in learning. The teacher can use various techniques to document how much students are currently engaged, collecting supporting evidence in a portfolio. The teacher can also use an instruction plan to analyze the activities for their potential to engage students in significant work. Next, the teacher can examine an instructional artifact (perhaps an assignment) and some

samples of student work resulting from that artifact. Lastly, a videotaped lesson can be analyzed to see the degree of student engagement in an instructional activity. The supervisor makes one or two classroom observations and documents examples of student engagement.

Then, with all the information in hand—contents of the teacher's portfolio and notes from the supervisor's observations—the two can engage in meaningful conversation. Together, they can determine the degree of student engagement in learning, with examples from the portfolio, including a videotape if possible, and from the supervisor's notes. If indicated, this is a good time to discuss alternative courses of action: what the teacher might have done at a particular point to enhance student engagement or how the assignment might have been structured to increase engagement.

CREATING A PROFESSIONAL DEVELOPMENT PLAN

The next step in the supervisory process is usually creating a professional development plan, or a professional improvement plan. This plan is based on the goals jointly determined and analyzed, together with agreed-upon steps to strengthen the identified skills. For example, the plan may contain a series of visits to other teachers' classrooms to observe their techniques for engaging students in learning, a workshop at a local agency, and books or a videotape in the school's professional library. This plan should be manageable—one that does not attempt to address too many components at one time and includes areas for which resources are available. Both the teacher and supervisor need to agree that the areas selected for attention are, indeed, the most critical and that the recommended steps will most likely result in the desired improvement.

Throughout this process, the teacher should continue to add items to a portfolio to demonstrate increasing skill in the identified components. A professional relationship with a mentor or peer coach enables the teacher to further strengthen these skills.

The Evaluation

The evaluation that results from a school using the framework is carried out according to established procedures. It documents the progress a teacher makes toward increasing skills in different components. The evaluation draws on documentation the teacher has collected in a portfolio as well as comments the supervisor has written. It comments on the progress made in implementing the professional improvement plan and the results achieved from that plan. The evaluation takes a long view of the teacher as a professional, one engaged in a process of continuing improvement.

6

The Framework for Professional Practice

This chapter describes the 22 components of professional practice within the framework of the four domains. The figure on the following page shows how the components are grouped under the domains. A description for each component has three parts: Rationale and Explanation, Documentation, and a figure showing the elements of the component and how the levels of performance apply to each element. There are four levels of performance: unsatisfactory, basic, proficient, and distinguished (see Chapter 3 for a general explanation of each performance level).

Components of Professional Practice

Domain 1: Planning and Preparation

Component 1a: Demonstrating Knowledge of Content and Pedagogy

Component 1b: Demonstrating Knowledge of Students

Component 1c: Selecting Instructional Goals

Component 1d: Demonstrating Knowledge of Resources

Component 1e: Designing Coherent Instruction

Component 1f: Assessing Student Learning

Domain 2: The Classroom Environment

Component 2a: Creating an Environment of Respect and Rapport

Component 2b: Establishing a Culture for Learning

Component 2c: Managing Classroom Procedures

Component 2d: Managing Student Behavior

Component 2e: Organizing Physical Space

Domain 3: Instruction

Component 3a: Communicating Clearly and Accurately

Component 3b: Using Questioning and Discussion Techniques

Component 3c: Engaging Students in Learning

Component 3d: Providing Feedback to Students

Component 3e: Demonstrating Flexibility and Responsiveness

Domain 4: Professional Responsibilities

Component 4a: Reflecting on Teaching

Component 4b: Maintaining Accurate Records

Component 4c: Communicating with Families

Component 4d: Contributing to the School and District

Component 4e: Growing and Developing Professionally

Component 4f: Showing Professionalism

DOMAIN 1: PLANNING AND PREPARATION

COMPONENT 1a:
DEMONSTRATING KNOWLEDGE OF CONTENT AND PEDAGOGY

Rationale and Explanation

"A person cannot teach what he or she does not know." This statement captures the essence of why content knowledge is important in teaching. Regardless of a teacher's instructional techniques, she must have sufficient command of a subject to guide student learning. This requirement is independent of a teacher's approach: Even those who embrace a constructivist or inquiry approach to instruction must understand the content to be learned, the structure of the discipline of which that content is a part, and the methods of inquiry unique to that discipline. Teachers must be aware of the connections among different divisions of the discipline (e.g., between writing and literature) and among the different disciplines themselves.

The term "content" includes, of course, far more than factual information. It encompasses all aspects of a subject: concepts, principles, relationships, methods of inquiry, and outstanding issues. Teachers who understand their subjects know which questions are likely to interest students, yield greater understanding, represent conceptual dead ends.

Students look to teachers as their source of information about a subject. Although teachers may sometimes withhold information to encourage student inquiry, what they do convey should be accurate.

Content must be presented so that it respects the nuances of a discipline. When engaging students in a discussion, teachers should show they understand the complexities and patterns of the content to be learned. For example, teachers of non-English languages should be able to speak with the appropriate accent. Teachers of physical education should be able to demonstrate or explain the skills they are teaching.

Although necessary for good teaching, subject knowledge is not enough. An example is the teacher who knows chemistry but cannot convey that knowledge or engage students in the subject. Teachers use pedagogical techniques particular to the different disciplines to help convey information and teach skills. Approaches used in writing, for example, may be very different from those in science. In addition, knowledgeable teachers know which concepts are central to a discipline and which are peripheral. Some disciplines, particularly mathematics, have important prerequisite relationships. For example, students must understand place value before they can understand addition and subtraction with regrouping. Other disciplines have similar internal constraints; students need to learn concepts or skills before they can tackle others. Knowledgeable teachers know where these important relationships are in the subjects they teach.

A teacher's knowledge of content and pedagogy is reflected in an awareness of common student misconceptions or likely sources of error—and how these should be handled. Elementary students, for example, sometimes confuse area and perimeter. A knowledgeable teacher recognizes that many students make this mistake and knows how to anticipate or correct it. Students may hold naive and incorrect concepts in science, such as how light is transmitted. Teachers who are knowledgeable about subject-based pedagogy anticipate such misconceptions and work to dispel them.

Certainly, knowledge of content and pedagogy is not stagnant but evolves over time. Even when teachers specialize at the university level in the disciplines they later teach, their knowledge, unless renewed, can become dated and stale. And if teachers' responsibilities for instruction change, they have an even greater need to become thoroughly acquainted with their new field or subfield. For example, suppose a teacher has been teaching high school chemistry for many years and switches to biology. That change will require content and pedagogical preparation in addition to that required if the teacher also continues to teach chemistry. Even teachers who stay with the same content must keep apprised of developments in the field and in the accepted best methods of engaging students with it.

Knowledge of content and pedagogy are appropriately different for teachers of different levels. Content specialists, who teach only one subject, may be held to a higher standard than generalists, who teach many subjects. Moreover, the balance between content and pedagogical knowledge varies from one discipline to another. In some disciplines, such as reading, the content does not change, but the pedagogy is critical. In others, such as science, both the content and the pedagogy change over time. That is, in reading, the instructional goal is for students to be able to derive meaning from written text. Although this goal has remained stable over many years, the approaches used (e.g., phonics and whole language) have been the subject of much controversy. Alternatively, science teachers must alter not only their instructional strategies over time but also the topics taught as new knowledge evolves.

Because of shifting enrollments, teachers are occasionally assigned to subjects or levels for which they have little professional preparation. When this happens, both the school and the teacher have a responsibility to remedy the deficiency.

Documentation

Teachers provide evidence of their evolving knowledge of content and pedagogy by developing instructional plans and participating in professional growth activities. Some examples of how teachers can demonstrate their commitment to remaining abreast of new developments follow:

• Preparing lessons based on recently accepted views of best practice (e.g., using a process approach to teach writing).

• Taking graduate-level courses in a discipline or in general teaching techniques.

• Taking an active role in adapting the new content standards and curriculum frameworks to their teaching.

Since many of these activities are not directly observable in the classroom, this component is primarily displayed through written documentation. Teachers can also display knowledge of the subjects they teach through instructional artifacts, comments on student work, and their classroom interactions with students. Content errors reflect a shaky understanding of the subject, and evasive responses to students may suggest only a thin knowledge of content. Some responses are deliberately unrevealing, though, because the teacher wants to engage students in their own investigations. When in doubt, an observer should ask the teacher if such responses are deliberate.

Figure 6.1				

DOMAIN I: PLANNING AND PREPARATION
Component 1a: Demonstrating Knowledge of Content and Pedagogy
Elements:
Knowledge of content • Knowledge of prerequisite relationships • Knowledge of content-related pedagogy

	LEVEL OF PERFORMANCE			
ELEMENT	UNSATISFACTORY	BASIC	PROFICIENT	DISTINGUISHED
Knowledge of Content	Teacher makes content errors or does not correct content errors students make.	Teacher displays basic content knowledge but cannot articulate connections with other parts of the discipline or with other disciplines.	Teacher displays solid content knowledge and makes connections between the content and other parts of the discipline and other disciplines.	Teacher displays extensive content knowledge, with evidence of continuing pursuit of such knowledge.
Knowledge of Prerequisite Relationships	Teacher displays little understanding of prerequisite knowledge important for student learning of the content.	Teacher indicates some awareness of prerequisite learning, although such knowledge may be incomplete or inaccurate.	Teacher's plans and practices reflect understanding of prerequisite relationships among topics and concepts.	Teacher actively builds on knowledge of prerequisite relationships when describing instruction or seeking causes for student misunderstanding.
Knowledge of Content-Related Pedagogy	Teacher displays little understanding of pedagogical issues involved in student learning of the content.	Teacher displays basic pedagogical knowledge but does not anticipate student misconceptions.	Pedagogical practices reflect current research on best pedagogical practice within the discipline but without anticipating student misconceptions.	Teacher displays continuing search for best practice and anticipates student misconceptions.

DOMAIN 1: PLANNING AND PREPARATION

COMPONENT 1b:
DEMONSTRATING KNOWLEDGE OF STUDENTS

Rationale and Explanation

Teachers do not teach their subjects in a vacuum; they teach them to students. To maximize learning, teachers must know not only their subject and its accompanying pedagogy, but also their students.

Each age group has certain developmental characteristics—intellectual, social, and emotional. Students in the late elementary and middle school years are learning skills related to friendship and peer relationships. The skill of separating and controlling variables in a scientific investigation is not present in most students until they are about 12. Recent research has verified the power and stability of students' misconceptions, particularly in mathematics and science. Teachers' knowledge of their students should include the students' stage of developmental understanding.

Current research on cognition states that understanding involves students in actively constructing meaning based on their experiences. Knowledge acquired through memorizing information and procedures is not permanent and is generally retained only until it is tested or until its use is ended. And if such knowledge is not fully understood, it is easily dislodged.

Because students are actively constructing meaning, they build their understanding on what they already know. For example, their current understanding of fractions influences what else they can learn and understand about the topic. Their current skill in writing influences the next steps in their basic competency. Some students may have erroneous information. Teachers' knowledge of students includes knowing what these misunderstandings and misconceptions are.

Students vary enormously in their interests, talents, and preferred approaches to learning. For example, many teachers know that an individual student is artistic, another is a whiz at numbers, and a third has highly creative ideas. Skilled teachers help students build on these strengths while developing all areas of competence.

Many classes contain students with special needs. Part of knowing students is knowing which ones require additional assistance in learning parts of the curriculum or which ones must demonstrate knowledge in unique ways. Teachers' knowledge of students should include information about such special cases, which is used in instructional planning.

Students' academic knowledge is not the only area that affects their experiences in learning. Students bring out-of-school knowledge of everyday events, interests, and activities, as well as misunderstandings and parents' opinions, to school with them. This knowledge influences school-based learning. For instance, students' understanding that a closed car becomes hot on a sunny but cold winter day, and that water sitting in a hose becomes very hot in the summer, can assist a teacher in introducing students to the workings of solar energy. Students may be active in sports, scouting, music, or drama. Such out-of-school experiences provide rich material for teachers in designing learning experiences and developing analogies and metaphors for new content.

Students come to the school environment with social and cultural characteristics that influence how they see the world, participate in learning activities, and absorb new information. For example, in some cultures, challenging an adult's authority is considered disrespectful. Children from these environments find it difficult to question a teacher's—or a textbook's—interpretation of, say, a historical event.

Documentation

Completing the Knowledge of Students and Resources Sheet (see Chapter 4) documents how teachers learn about students' background knowledge and skills, interests outside school, cultural heritage, and special needs. This knowledge is also evident in the learning experiences teachers create for their students.

Figure 6.2

DOMAIN 1: PLANNING AND PREPARATION
Component 1b: Demonstrating Knowledge of Students
Elements:
Knowledge of characteristics (intellectual, social, and emotional) of age group • Knowledge of students' varied approaches to learning • Knowledge of students' skills and knowledge • Knowledge of students' interests and cultural heritage

ELEMENT	LEVEL OF PERFORMANCE			
	UNSATISFACTORY	BASIC	PROFICIENT	DISTINGUISHED
Knowledge of Characteristics of Age Group	Teacher displays minimal knowledge of developmental characteristics of age group.	Teacher displays generally accurate knowledge of developmental characteristics of age group.	Teacher displays thorough understanding of typical developmental characteristics of age group as well as exceptions to general patterns.	Teacher displays knowledge of typical developmental characteristics of age group, exceptions to the patterns, and the extent to which each student follows patterns.
Knowledge of Students' Varied Approaches to Learning	Teacher is unfamiliar with the different approaches to learning that students exhibit, such as learning styles, modalities, and different "intelligences."	Teacher displays general understanding of the different approaches to learning that students exhibit.	Teacher displays solid understanding of the different approaches to learning that different students exhibit.	Teacher uses, where appropriate, knowledge of students' varied approaches to learning in instructional planning.
Knowledge of Students' Skills and Knowledge	Teacher displays little knowledge of students' skills and knowledge and does not indicate that such knowledge is valuable.	Teacher recognizes the value of understanding students' skills and knowledge but displays this knowledge for the class only as a whole.	Teacher displays knowledge of students' skills and knowledge for groups of students and recognizes the value of this knowledge.	Teacher displays knowledge of students' skills and knowledge for each student, including those with special needs.
Knowledge of Students' Interests and Cultural Heritage	Teacher displays little knowledge of students' interests or cultural heritage and does not indicate that such knowledge is valuable.	Teacher recognizes the value of understanding students' interests or cultural heritage but displays this knowledge for the class only as a whole.	Teacher displays knowledge of the interests or cultural heritage of groups of students and recognizes the value of this knowledge.	Teacher displays knowledge of the interests or cultural heritage of each student.

DOMAIN 1: PLANNING AND PREPARATION

COMPONENT 1c:
SELECTING INSTRUCTIONAL GOALS

Rationale and Explanation

Teaching is a purposeful activity—it is goal directed, designed to achieve certain well-defined purposes. These purposes should be clear.

In general, it is a teacher's responsibility to establish instructional goals. In classrooms organized as a community of learners, however, teachers engage students in determining these goals. As students assume increasingly greater responsibility for their own learning, they select their own learning tasks in pursuit of shared goals.

When teachers establish instructional goals, they must take into account a number of factors: a district's curriculum (generally grounded in state or discipline-based curriculum frameworks), the requirements of external mandates (e.g., state-testing or voluntary programs such as Advanced Placement examinations), and community expectations.

Instructional goals must be worthwhile and represent learning central to a discipline as well as high-level learning for the students. Not all knowledge and skill in a discipline are worth learning; trivial facts, although they may be true, are of little value. In selecting instructional goals, teachers should consider the importance of what they introduce to students.

Instructional goals must be clear and stated in terms of student learning rather than student activity: "What will students *learn* as a result of the instructional engagement?" Not, "What will students do?" There can be many types of instructional goals, and they may reflect diverse long-range purposes of schooling. The goals may deal with knowledge and understanding, thinking, or social skills. Indeed, content and process goals are usually present simultaneously; far from being in conflict with one another, they complement and build on one another. That instructional goals are clearly stated does not imply that they should be low level in their cognitive challenge.

Instructional goals should be capable of assessment. They must be stated in clear language that permits viable methods of evaluation and the establishment of performance standards. Verbs that define instructional goals should be unambiguous and suggest assessment techniques. For example, the goal, "The student will write for a variety of purposes and audiences," is too general to suggest assessment methodologies or standards of performance. It is satisfactory as a broad program goal or outcome; however, for instructional planning and assessment, it should be narrowed, tightened, and illustrated with a sample of student work.

The goals must be appropriate to the diverse students in a teacher's charge, providing for the students' age and developmental levels, prior skills and knowledge, and interests and backgrounds. Not all goals are equally suitable for all students, nor are the same goals always appropriate for all students in a class. Skilled teachers adjust their instructional goals to accommodate the diversity represented by their students.

Together, instructional goals should reflect a balance among different types of learning. Some may represent factual knowledge or conceptual understanding. Others may include reasoning skills, social skills, or communication. Still others may include dispositions, such as a willingness to listen to all points of view or taking pride in one's work. A single lesson may incorporate only a few types of goals; a longer unit generally includes a balance.

Documentation

Teachers state their instructional goals and describe how the goals relate to district curriculum guidelines, state frameworks, content standards, and curriculum goals in a discipline on the Instruction Plan for a Single Lesson (see Chapter 4). They can also explain how the goals are appropriate for their students. Further indication of a teacher's skill in establishing instructional goals can be derived from conversations with the teacher, either before or after a lesson is observed. The suitability of instructional goals for a diverse group of students is best observed during a classroom visit.

Figure 6.3

DOMAIN I: PLANNING AND PREPARATION
Component 1c: Selecting Instructional Goals
Elements:

VALUE: Goals represent high expectations for students; and reflect important learning and conceptual understanding, curriculum standards, and frameworks. • CLARITY: Goals are clearly stated as student learning and permit sound assessment. • SUITABILITY FOR DIVERSE STUDENTS: Goals reflect needs of all students in a class. • BALANCE: Goals represent opportunities for different types of learning—for example, thinking as well as knowledge—and coordination or integration within or across disciplines.

LEVEL OF PERFORMANCE

ELEMENT	UNSATISFACTORY	BASIC	PROFICIENT	DISTINGUISHED
Value	Goals are not valuable and represent low expectations or no conceptual understanding for students. Goals do not reflect important learning.	Goals are moderately valuable in either their expectations or conceptual understanding for students and in importance of learning.	Goals are valuable in their level of expectations, conceptual understanding, and importance of learning.	Not only are the goals valuable, but teacher can also clearly articulate how goals establish high expectations and relate to curriculum frameworks and standards.
Clarity	Goals are either not clear or are stated as student activities. Goals do not permit viable methods of assessment.	Goals are only moderately clear or include a combination of goals and activities. Some goals do not permit viable methods of assessment.	Most of the goals are clear but may include a few activities. Most permit viable methods of assessment.	All the goals are clear, written in the form of student learning, and permit viable methods of assessment.
Suitability for Diverse Students	Goals are not suitable for the class.	Most of the goals are suitable for most students in the class.	All the goals are suitable for most students in the class.	Goals take into account the varying learning needs of individual students or groups.
Balance	Goals reflect only one type of learning and one discipline or strand.	Goals reflect several types of learning but no effort at coordination or integration.	Goals reflect several different types of learning and opportunities for integration.	Goals reflect student initiative in establishing important learning.

DOMAIN 1: PLANNING AND PREPARATION

COMPONENT 1d:
DEMONSTRATING KNOWLEDGE OF RESOURCES

Rationale and Explanation

There are two primary types of resources: those to assist in teaching and those to help students. Although the balance between the two types varies in different settings, both should be, to some degree, evident in all contexts.

Resources for teaching include the myriad things used in any classroom; they may be simple or complex and purchased or made by the teacher or students. Resources also include aids outside the classroom, such as museums, concert performances, and materials from local businesses. Teachers can draw from a wide variety of human resources, from experts within the classroom community (students and parents), to those from the larger business and civic world. Some resources are available from a school or district, such as texts. Most teachers extend their reach for instructional materials beyond what a school provides, thereby enhancing their students' experiences.

When teachers are knowledgeable about the range of resources to aid in their teaching, they can expand their repertoire of instructional goals, knowing that they can go to these resources for help.

Awareness of these resources is the first step in using them in a classroom.

Knowledge of resources to assist students is part of all teachers' responsibility. Students' full potential can only be realized if their teachers are aware of what is available. Resources for students include items and services available both through and beyond the school. These resources can take the form of special services, such as an instructional aide to help a hearing-impaired student. Resources may include a range of offerings within a regular school setting, for example, resource room assistance for learning disabled students at the elementary level or courses geared for different levels of challenge at the secondary level. Some outside resources help academic learning: tutoring services and homework hot lines. Others meet non-academic needs: Big Brother and Big Sister programs and mentoring programs. Most communities sponsor agencies to help students who have acute physical needs (e.g., providing winter coats and shoes) and students who are victims of physical or sexual abuse or who themselves abuse alcohol or drugs.

Documentation

Information about teachers' knowledge of resources is shown primarily on the Knowledge of Students and Resources Sheet (see Chapter 4).

Figure 6.4	**DOMAIN 1: PLANNING AND PREPARATION** **Component 1d: Demonstrating Knowledge of Resources** *Elements:* *Resources for teaching • Resources for students*

	LEVEL OF PERFORMANCE			
ELEMENT	UNSATISFACTORY	BASIC	PROFICIENT	DISTINGUISHED
Resources for Teaching	Teacher is unaware of resources available through the school or district.	Teacher displays limited awareness of resources available through the school or district.	Teacher is fully aware of all resources available through the school or district.	In addition to being aware of school and district resources, teacher actively seeks other materials to enhance instruction, for example, from professional organizations or through the community.
Resources for Students	Teacher is unaware of resources available to assist students who need them.	Teacher displays limited awareness of resources available through the school or district.	Teacher is fully aware of all resources available through the school or district and knows how to gain access for students.	In addition to being aware of school and district resources, teacher is aware of additional resources available through the community.

DOMAIN 1: PLANNING AND PREPARATION

COMPONENT 1e:
DESIGNING COHERENT INSTRUCTION

Rationale and Explanation

A teacher translates instructional goals into learning experiences for students through the design of instruction. Even in classrooms where students assume considerable responsibility for their learning, the teacher is in charge of organizing the environment, managing the learning process, and establishing the framework for investigations.

Since instructional goals are varied, the choice of instructional strategies is also likely to vary. For example, the methods used in helping students understand a routine procedure, such as how to clean laboratory glassware, are likely to be different from those used in enabling students to engage in independent projects. Some lessons consist of presentations, while others are more like workshops, with a teacher's role correspondingly different.

A critical element in instructional design is the creation or adaptation of a series of learning activities within an instructional unit. This sequence should be logical and likely to engage students in meaningful activities. The activities should progress from easier to harder, simple to more complex, from attention to one domain of learning to integration across several. The activities should be suitable to students in terms of their age, prior knowledge and interests, and approaches to learning. The activities and grouping strategies should vary, showing many ways to engage students in the content. Small-group work and reporting out may be an effective approach, but as a steady diet, such activity will become tedious.

Another element in instructional design is the choice of materials and resources. Teachers should select these carefully and make sure they clearly support the instructional goals. Materials and resources also need to engage students in meaningful learning; hence, directions and guidelines for a project are likely to yield higher quality student learning than a fill-in-the-blanks worksheet.

Compatibility with recent research findings that are reported in professional journals and reflected in the content standards and frameworks is another important element of good instructional design. For example, with the National Council of Teachers of Mathematics standards and many state curriculum guides urging a problem-solving approach to the teaching of mathematics, coherent instruction should reflect such an orientation. Similarly, educators are urged to engage students in the "doing" of science and in investigating history topics in depth.

A coherent instructional unit has a well-defined structure. Individual activities support the whole, each activity playing an important role. Time allocations are reasonable, with opportunities for students to engage in reflection and closure. Topics from one part of the unit are connected with others; students explore a subject from many different angles and understand the relationship of the parts to the whole. Instructional groups are suitable to both the instructional goals and the students. Where appropriate, students themselves take some initiative in choosing their own work group.

Documentation

Planning for coherent instruction is demonstrated by a unit plan encompassing several weeks. That time span enables teachers to demonstrate their skill in organizing and sequencing activities to engage students in learning, in using a variety of materials and groups appropriately, and in allocating reasonable time. This planning skill is best demonstrated through the Three-Week Unit Plan. The Instruction Plan for a Single Lesson reveals detailed planning and enables observers to see the coherence of that instructional event (see Chapter 4 for both plans).

Figure 6.5

DOMAIN 1: PLANNING AND PREPARATION
Component 1e: Designing Coherent Instruction
Elements:
Learning activities • Instructional materials and resources • Instructional groups • Lesson and unit structure

	LEVEL OF PERFORMANCE			
ELEMENT	UNSATISFACTORY	BASIC	PROFICIENT	DISTINGUISHED
Learning Activities	Learning activities are not suitable to students or instructional goals. They do not follow an organized progression and do not reflect recent professional research.	Only some of the learning activities are suitable to students or instructional goals. Progression of activities in the unit is uneven, and only some activities reflect recent professional research.	Most of the learning activities are suitable to students and instructional goals. Progression of activities in the unit is fairly even, and most activities reflect recent professional research.	Learning activities are highly relevant to students and instructional goals. They progress coherently, producing a unified whole and reflecting recent professional research.
Instructional Materials and Resources	Materials and resources do not support the instructional goals or engage students in meaningful learning.	Some of the materials and resources support the instructional goals, and some engage students in meaningful learning.	All materials and resources support the instructional goals, and most engage students in meaningful learning.	All materials and resources support the instructional goals, and most engage students in meaningful learning. There is evidence of student participation in selecting or adapting materials.
Instructional Groups	Instructional groups do not support the instructional goals and offer no variety.	Instructional groups are inconsistent in suitability to the instructional goals and offer minimal variety.	Instructional groups are varied, as appropriate to the different instructional goals.	Instructional groups are varied, as appropriate to the different instructional goals. There is evidence of student choice in selecting different patterns of instructional groups.
Lesson and Unit Structure	The lesson or unit has no clearly defined structure, or the structure is chaotic. Time allocations are unrealistic.	The lesson or unit has a recognizable structure, although the structure is not uniformly maintained throughout. Most time allocations are reasonable.	The lesson or unit has a clearly defined structure that activities are organized around. Time allocations are reasonable.	The lesson's or unit's structure is clear and allows for different pathways according to student needs.

DOMAIN 1: PLANNING AND PREPARATION

COMPONENT 1f: ASSESSING STUDENT LEARNING

Rationale and Explanation

Only through the assessment of student learning can teachers know if students have met the instructional goals of a unit or lesson. The more diverse the types of instructional goals, the more diverse the approaches to assessment must be.

One requirement of a design for assessing student learning is that each instructional goal can be assessed in some way. Moreover, the assessment methodologies must be appropriate to the different types of goals. For example, a science unit may contain seven instructional goals: one relates to factual knowledge, one to conceptual understanding, two to data analysis, two to communication of findings, and one to collaboration skills. Clearly, no single approach is suitable for all these goals. A simple factual test may be appropriate for the factual knowledge; but for conceptual understanding, data analysis, communication of findings, and collaboration skills, other approaches are necessary.

A well-designed approach is clear about how student work will be evaluated. Again, this type of evaluation is relatively easy with a test in which questions have a single right answer, student responses can be counted, and percentages calculated. But for more complex instructional goals, and for assessment methods that don't yield a

single correct response, part of designing an assessment is to determine a scoring system, or a rubric for evaluating student work.

Such a rubric not only identifies the criteria of an acceptable response but also establishes standards of performance. An example is an instructional goal that states, "Students will write a descriptive essay." For the goal to be meaningful, a teacher needs to define the length and organization of the essay, attention needed for the mechanics, and use of language.

If possible, students should know the required standards of achievement. Secrecy has no role in assessment—such an environment feels like "gotcha" to students. Of course, the exact questions that will appear on an assessment should not be given to students in advance. But there is no reason they can't be informed about the *type* of questions that will be asked and the content to be covered. Then, by studying that content and by reviewing exemplary responses to sample items, students can better prepare for the assessment.

Assessment methodologies ideally should reflect authentic, real-world applications of knowledge and understanding. Although not always possible, such authenticity motivates students and provides teachers with excellent insight into student learning.

Some schools collect student work in a portfolio and use that as the basis for assessment and future placement, for example, in advanced courses. Such an approach requires carefully considering what goes into the portfolio and the criteria used in evaluating each piece of work.

The full power of assessment is its use in providing feedback to students (Component 3d), reflecting on teaching (Component 4a), and planning for the future (Component 1f). When used to inform the instructional process and plans for next steps, assessment becomes integral to the act of teaching.

Documentation

Teachers' skill in assessing student learning is demonstrated primarily through the Instruction Plan for a Single Lesson (see Chapter 4).

Figure 6.6

DOMAIN 1: PLANNING AND PREPARATION
Component 1f: Assessing Student Learning
Elements:
Congruence with instructional goals • Criteria and standards • Use for planning

	LEVEL OF PERFORMANCE			
ELEMENT	UNSATISFACTORY	BASIC	PROFICIENT	DISTINGUISHED
Congruence with Instructional Goals	Content and methods of assessment lack congruence with instructional goals.	Some of the instructional goals are assessed through the proposed approach, but many are not.	All the instructional goals are nominally assessed through the proposed plan, but the approach is more suitable to some goals than to others.	The proposed approach to assessment is completely congruent with the instructional goals, both in content and process.
Criteria and Standards	The proposed approach contains no clear criteria or standards.	Assessment criteria and standards have been developed, but they are either not clear or have not been clearly communicated to students.	Assessment criteria and standards are clear and have been clearly communicated to students.	Assessment criteria and standards are clear and have been clearly communicated to students. There is evidence that students contributed to the development of the criteria and standards.
Use for Planning	The assessment results affect planning for these students only minimally.	Teacher uses assessment results to plan for the class as a whole.	Teacher uses assessment results to plan for individuals and groups of students.	Students are aware of how they are meeting the established standards and participate in planning the next steps.

DOMAIN 2: THE CLASSROOM ENVIRONMENT

COMPONENT 2a: CREATING AN ENVIRONMENT OF RESPECT AND RAPPORT

Rationale and Explanation

Teaching is a matter of relationships among individuals. These relationships should be grounded in rapport and mutual respect, both between a teacher and students and among students.

Teachers create an environment of respect and rapport in their classrooms by the ways they interact with students and by the interaction they encourage and cultivate among students. In a respectful environment, *all* students feel valued and safe. They know they will be treated with dignity, even when they take intellectual risks. High levels of respect and rapport are sometimes characterized by friendliness and openness, and frequently by humor, but never by a teacher forgetting her role as an adult.

Sometimes, teachers convey their caring for students through a somewhat stern demeanor and businesslike atmosphere. Underneath, however, is the essential *caring* that teachers exhibit for their students and the caring that students are encouraged to exhibit for one another.

Lack of respect and rapport are demonstrated in many ways. Teachers may disregard or demean some students' contributions. They may use sarcasm and put-downs, or they may permit students to engage in similar behavior. Teachers may show favoritism or be inappropriately friendly or pals with their students.

Appropriate ways of demonstrating respect and rapport reflect the context and depend on nonverbal as well as verbal behavior. What is suitable for kindergarten children is unusual, or even inappropriate, for high school students. Parts of student-teacher interaction may be influenced by the cultural traditions of students; for example, ways of showing respect in one environment may be offensive in another.

Documentation

Teachers demonstrate skill in establishing an environment of respect and rapport through their words and actions in the classroom. Occasionally, interaction with a student may require that a teacher offer an explanation so that an observer can fully understand the teacher's actions. Such explanations can take place in a discussion following the class.

Figure 6.7	**DOMAIN 2: THE CLASSROOM ENVIRONMENT** **Component 2a: Creating an Environment of Respect and Rapport** *Elements:* *Teacher interaction with students • Student interaction*			
	L E V E L O F P E R F O R M A N C E			
ELEMENT	UNSATISFACTORY	BASIC	PROFICIENT	DISTINGUISHED
Teacher Interaction with Students	Teacher interaction with at least some students is negative, demeaning, sarcastic, or inappropriate to the age or culture of the students. Students exhibit disrespect for teacher.	Teacher-student interactions are generally appropriate but may reflect occasional inconsistencies, favoritism, or disregard for students' cultures. Students exhibit only minimal respect for teacher.	Teacher-student interactions are friendly and demonstrate general warmth, caring, and respect. Such interactions are appropriate to developmental and cultural norms. Students exhibit respect for teacher.	Teacher demonstrates genuine caring and respect for individual students. Students exhibit respect for teacher as an individual, beyond that for the role.
Student Interaction	Student interactions are characterized by conflict, sarcasm, or put-downs.	Students do not demonstrate negative behavior toward one another.	Student interactions are generally polite and respectful.	Students demonstrate genuine caring for one another as individuals and as students.

DOMAIN 2: THE CLASSROOM ENVIRONMENT

COMPONENT 2b:
ESTABLISHING A CULTURE FOR LEARNING

Rationale and Explanation

In classrooms with a strong culture for learning, everyone, including the teacher, is engaged in pursuits of value. Rather than an atmosphere of "getting by," or "punching the time clock," both students and teachers take pride in their work and give it their best energy. In such classrooms, it is "cool" to be smart, and good ideas are valued.

A culture for learning implies high expectations for all students and a safe environment for taking risks. Students know that they do not have to fear ridicule when they advance an idea and that their teachers will ensure that their ideas receive a thoughtful reception. Moreover, students know that their teacher has a high regard for their abilities, and they are strengthened in their commitment to high-quality work. These high expectations, which students internalize and convey, are at the heart of a culture for learning.

Classrooms without a culture for learning are characterized by an atmosphere where no one—teacher or students—cares about the content to be learned. The teacher may even indirectly blame the textbook, the administration, the state, or the district for a curriculum that she doesn't think has much value. Students are lethargic or alienated, do not invest energy in their work, and appear motivated by the desire to get by, preferably with as little effort as possible.

On the other hand, classrooms with a culture for learning are cognitively busy places, with students and teacher setting a high value on high-quality work. Student work may be displayed, and student-teacher interactions are characterized by teacher insistence on and student acceptance of the need for students to expend their best efforts. Both students and teacher see the content as important, and students take obvious pride in their work.

Students, as well as the teacher, demonstrate that a culture for learning has been established. Such a culture is highly dependent on factors outside the school. For example, some families value education more than do others. Nevertheless, teachers have a responsibility to create such an atmosphere in their classrooms.

A culture for learning can be established in every classroom. Schoolwide commitment to the culture greatly strengthens the classroom environment. And formal and informal school norms, from awards and assemblies, to recognition by the principal, to displays of student work in hallways and other public spaces, reinforce the commitment. Such a school demonstrates high levels of intellectual energy, extending beyond the specific demands of the school curriculum.

Documentation

Evidence of a culture for learning is found primarily in the classroom itself, where it's evident from the look of the room (which shows student work), nature of the interactions, and tone of the conversations. Teachers' instructional goals and activities, described in the Instruction Plan for a Single Lesson (see Chapter 4), also document high expectations for learning of all students. Conversations with students reveal that they value learning and hard work.

		DOMAIN 2: THE CLASSROOM ENVIRONMENT		

Figure 6.8

DOMAIN 2: THE CLASSROOM ENVIRONMENT
Component 2b: Establishing a Culture for Learning
Elements:
Importance of the content • Student pride in work • Expectations for learning and achievement

LEVEL OF PERFORMANCE

ELEMENT	UNSATISFACTORY	BASIC	PROFICIENT	DISTINGUISHED
Importance of the Content	Teacher or students convey a negative attitude toward the content, suggesting that the content is not important or is mandated by others.	Teacher communicates importance of the work but with little conviction and only minimal apparent buy-in by the students.	Teacher conveys genuine enthusiasm for the subject, and students demonstrate consistent commitment to its value.	Students demonstrate through their active participation, curiosity, and attention to detail that they value the content's importance.
Student Pride in Work	Students demonstrate little or no pride in their work. They seem to be motivated by the desire to complete a task rather than do high-quality work.	Students minimally accept the responsibility to "do good work" but invest little of their energy in the quality of the work.	Students accept teacher insistence on work of high quality and demonstrate pride in that work.	Students take obvious pride in their work and initiate improvements in it, for example, by revising drafts on their own initiative, helping peers, and ensuring that high-quality work is displayed.
Expectations for Learning and Achievement	Instructional goals and activities, interactions, and the classroom environment convey only modest expectations for student achievement.	Instructional goals and activities, interactions, and the classroom environment convey inconsistent expectations for student achievement.	Instructional goals and activities, interactions, and the classroom environment convey high expectations for student achievement.	Both students and teacher establish and maintain through planning of learning activities, interactions, and the classroom environment high expectations for the learning of all students.

DOMAIN 2: THE CLASSROOM ENVIRONMENT

COMPONENT 2c:
MANAGING CLASSROOM PROCEDURES

Rationale and Explanation

Teaching requires good management before good instruction is possible. The best instructional techniques are worthless in an environment of chaos. Therefore, teachers find that they must develop procedures for the smooth operation of the classroom and the efficient use of time before they can address instructional techniques. Routines are established for the movement and management of classroom groups, distribution and collection of materials, performance of noninstructional responsibilities, and supervision of volunteers and paraprofessionals. Students understand where they are to go and what they are to do, with minimal confusion.

A poorly managed classroom is easy to spot: Time is wasted in noninstructional matters, students must wait for a teacher's attention, instructional groups are off-task, materials are not at hand, and transitions are confused. In a well-managed classroom, procedures and transitions are seamless, and students assume responsibility for the classroom's smooth operation. Instructional groups are engaged at all times, and students function well in those groups. Even when the teacher is not directly monitoring their activities, students working in groups maintain their momentum, seeking help when they need it.

Experienced teachers demonstrate their skill in managing smooth transitions: Different activities have clear beginnings and endings, and minimal time is lost as the teacher and students move from one lesson segment to another. Materials needed for instruction are at hand, and procedures for distributing and collecting materials are well established and followed. Students assume responsibility for the care and location of materials, which are easily found.

Experienced teachers devise routine techniques for expediting the myriad noninstructional duties for which they are responsible, leaving maximum time for instruction. Little time is lost in taking attendance or lunch count, collecting permission slips, and organizing extracurricular activities.

Classroom volunteers and paraprofessionals can greatly enhance the quality of a program, but they generally require a considerable amount of supervision before they can make much of a contribution. Experienced teachers devote the necessary time to providing guidance to their assistants. As a result, they ensure that those assistants can make a substantial contribution to the class.

Documentation

Evidence for how teachers manage classroom procedures is obtained through classroom observation. Most teachers also explain their procedures.

Figure 6.9

DOMAIN 2: THE CLASSROOM ENVIRONMENT
Component 2c: Managing Classroom Procedures
Elements:
Management of instructional groups • Management of transitions • Management of materials and supplies
Performance of noninstructional duties • Supervision of volunteers and paraprofessionals

ELEMENT	LEVEL OF PERFORMANCE			
	UNSATISFACTORY	BASIC	PROFICIENT	DISTINGUISHED
Management of Instructional Groups	Students not working with the teacher are not productively engaged in learning.	Tasks for group work are partially organized, resulting in some off-task behavior when teacher is involved with one group.	Tasks for group work are organized, and groups are managed so most students are engaged at all times.	Groups working independently are productively engaged at all times, with students assuming responsibility for productivity.
Management of Transitions	Much time is lost during transitions.	Transitions are sporadically efficient, resulting in some loss of instructional time.	Transitions occur smoothly, with little loss of instructional time.	Transitions are seamless, with students assuming some responsibility for efficient operation.
Management of Materials and Supplies	Materials are handled inefficiently, resulting in loss of instructional time.	Routines for handling materials and supplies function moderately well.	Routines for handling materials and supplies occur smoothly, with little loss of instructional time.	Routines for handling materials and supplies are seamless, with students assuming some responsibility for efficient operation.
Performance of Non-instructional Duties	Considerable instructional time is lost in performing noninstructional duties.	Systems for performing noninstructional duties are fairly efficient, resulting in little loss of instructional time.	Efficient systems for performing noninstructional duties are in place, resulting in minimal loss of instructional time.	Systems for performing noninstructional duties are well established, with students assuming considerable responsibility for efficient operation.
Supervision of Volunteers and Paraprofessionals	Volunteers and paraprofessionals have no clearly defined duties or do nothing most of the time.	Volunteers and paraprofessionals are productively engaged during portions of class time but require frequent supervision.	Volunteers and paraprofessionals are productively and independently engaged during the entire class.	Volunteers and paraprofessionals make a substantive contribution to the classroom environment.

DOMAIN 2: THE CLASSROOM ENVIRONMENT

COMPONENT 2d:
MANAGING STUDENT BEHAVIOR

Rationale and Explanation

Learning cannot occur in an environment where student behavior is out of control. If students are running around, defying the teacher, or picking fights, they cannot also engage deeply with content. Of course, the reverse is also true: When students are engaged deeply with content, they are less likely to pick fights, defy a teacher, or run around a classroom.

Most classrooms are crowded places, with students sharing space and materials. This proximity, exacerbated by other elements, can cause students to be disruptive. Experienced teachers recognize that much of what appears to be student misbehavior is actually a result of other causes:

• Students who are not prepared attempt to camouflage their situation by "acting out."

• Students who find a task unengaging let their attention wander to more interesting matters. For example, high school students pass notes or discuss out-of-class events; a 2nd grader converts his pencil to a "car" and runs it around his desk, with appropriate sound effects.

• Students who have poorly developed social skills and low self-esteem find opportunities to initiate oral and physical confrontations with other students, disrupting a class.

A key to efficient and respectful management of student behavior lies in agreed-upon standards of conduct and clear consequences for overstepping the bounds. Such standards may encompass appropriate language (e.g., no swearing), attire (e.g., no hats), and various procedures: for being recognized to speak during a discussion (e.g., raise hand or other signal for the discussion leader), for entering and leaving the classroom (e.g., lining up or dismissal by rows), for sharpening pencils, for getting materials, and for going to the rest room.

Whatever the details of the standards of conduct, approaches to managing student behavior in well-run classrooms share certain characteristics:

• Expectations are clear to everyone and may be posted in a classroom.

• The standards of behavior are appropriate to the developmental levels of the students and are consistent with the cultural norms of students in the class.

• Expectations are consistently applied—no favoritism.

• Teachers are aware of what is going on; they have "eyes in the backs of their heads." Teachers sometimes influence students, for example, by calling on a student to redirect her attention or by moving nearer to a student.

• Teachers refrain from losing their temper, banging books on a desk, or otherwise demonstrating that they have lost their composure. Students do not fear being physically or orally attacked.

• Any chastisement of conduct focuses on a student's behavior, not on the student. It is carried out so that the classroom rhythm is only minimally disrupted and the student's dignity is maintained.

• Teachers encourage students to monitor their own behavior.

Documentation

A teacher's skill in managing student behavior must be observed in the classroom. Standards of conduct, however, must frequently be inferred because in a smoothly running classroom, an observer may not witness explicit attention to those standards. Rather, student behavior indicates that a teacher has established standards at the beginning of the year and has maintained them consistently. Even though most teachers can also articulate their approach to standards of conduct, implementation is critical.

Figure 6.10

DOMAIN 2: THE CLASSROOM ENVIRONMENT
Component 2d: Managing Student Behavior
Elements:
Expectations • Monitoring of student behavior • Response to student misbehavior

ELEMENT	LEVEL OF PERFORMANCE			
	UNSATISFACTORY	BASIC	PROFICIENT	DISTINGUISHED
Expectations	No standards of conduct appear to have been established, or students are confused as to what the standards are.	Standards of conduct appear to have been established for most situations, and most students seem to understand them.	Standards of conduct are clear to all students.	Standards of conduct are clear to all students and appear to have been developed with student participation.
Monitoring of Student Behavior	Student behavior is not monitored, and teacher is unaware of what students are doing.	Teacher is generally aware of student behavior but may miss the activities of some students.	Teacher is alert to student behavior at all times.	Monitoring by teacher is subtle and preventive. Students monitor their own and their peers' behavior, correcting one another respectfully.
Response to Student Misbehavior	Teacher does not respond to misbehavior, or the response is inconsistent, overly repressive, or does not respect the student's dignity.	Teacher attempts to respond to student misbehavior but with uneven results, or no serious disruptive behavior occurs.	Teacher response to misbehavior is appropriate and successful and respects the student's dignity, or student behavior is generally appropriate.	Teacher response to misbehavior is highly effective and sensitive to students' individual needs, or student behavior is entirely appropriate.

DOMAIN 2: THE CLASSROOM ENVIRONMENT

COMPONENT 2e: ORGANIZING PHYSICAL SPACE

Rationale and Explanation

Use of physical space is important in a total learning environment and varies depending on context. Elementary teachers establish "reading corners" and spaces for noisy and quiet activities, and teachers at all levels create furniture arrangements for discussion sessions or group projects. Organization of space sends signals to students about how teachers view learning: "centers" for exploration, desks facing forward for a presentation, chairs in a circle for a group discussion, or a science lab organized in a businesslike manner.

One element of a physical environment concerns safety and accessibility to learning. A classroom must be safe—no dangling cords or obstructed exits. Students, including those with special needs, must have accessibility to the board, the teacher, and other learning resources. A physical environment must also accommodate efficient traffic flow. For example, all students must be able to get to a pencil sharpener and other materials and resources.

A second element involves the arrangement of furniture. Few desks are now bolted to the floor, although many teachers still want chairs or desks arranged in rows and columns. Depending on the instructional goals and the type of student activity planned, such an arrangement may not be optimal. For group work, tables or desks arranged in blocks may be preferable. And if students are expected to discuss ideas with each other, they need to be able to see one another. For a class discussion, desks or chairs arranged in a circle may be best.

A final element is teachers' use of physical resources. Teaching aids, such as chalkboards, flip charts, overhead projectors, and VCRs, may be skillfully or poorly used. When used well, they enhance learning and contribute to effective instruction. When used poorly, they detract from learning—machines that don't work mean that transparencies are out of focus or can't be read, or videos can't be seen.

When a classroom is a true community of learners, students themselves become involved in the physical environment and take initiative in making it effective. They may, for example, plan a display of work, move furniture to facilitate a group project, or shift supplies to improve traffic flow. They may lower the shades to block the sun from a classmate's eyes or shut the door to keep out hall noise. It is their room, and they make it work. Naturally, such student involvement can only occur when the teacher cultivates and encourages student participation in establishing the environment.

Some teachers, such as itinerant teachers, have only limited control over the physical environment in which they teach. All teachers must be responsible for a safe environment, but they can only be held accountable for the parts of their work they can control.

Documentation

Teachers' use of the physical environment must be observed. Teachers may be able to explain how they enhance the physical environment and use it as a resource for learning, but implementation is essential.

Figure 6.11

DOMAIN 2: THE CLASSROOM ENVIRONMENT
Component 2e: Organizing Physical Space
Elements:
Safety and arrangement of furniture • Accessibility to learning and use of physical resources

	LEVEL OF PERFORMANCE			
ELEMENT	UNSATISFACTORY	BASIC	PROFICIENT	DISTINGUISHED
Safety and Arrangement of Furniture	The classroom is unsafe, or the furniture arrangement is not suited to the lesson activities, or both.	The classroom is safe, and classroom furniture is adjusted for a lesson, or if necessary, a lesson is adjusted to the furniture, but with limited effectiveness.	The classroom is safe, and the furniture arrangement is a resource for learning activities.	The classroom is safe, and students adjust the furniture to advance their own purposes in learning.
Accessibility to Learning and Use of Physical Resources	Teacher uses physical resources poorly, or learning is not accessible to some students.	Teacher uses physical resources adequately, and at least essential learning is accessible to all students.	Teacher uses physical resources skillfully, and all learning is equally accessible to all students.	Both teacher and students use physical resources optimally, and students ensure that all learning is equally accessible to all students.

DOMAIN 3: INSTRUCTION

COMPONENT 3a:
COMMUNICATING CLEARLY AND ACCURATELY

Rationale and Explanation

For students to become engaged in learning, they must be exposed to clear directions and explanations. In addition, a teacher's use of vivid and expressive language can enhance a learning experience. Clear and accurate communication has two elements.

The first element is clarity of directions and procedures. When students work independently or in small groups, the information they receive must be clear. Otherwise, valuable time is lost while they are confused or are engaged in the wrong activity. Clear directions may be given orally, in writing, or a combination of the two. When students are determining their own procedures or activities, for example, in an art project, a teacher should make clear any limits to their choices.

The second element is the quality of oral and written communication. Because teachers communicate to students largely through language, that language must be audible and legible. When teachers speak, students must be able to hear and understand; when teachers distribute written directions, students must be able to read and understand them.

Students may model their use of language on that of their teachers. Consequently, teachers' language should reflect correct usage and contain expressive vocabulary. Not all oral communication needs to be expressed formally at all times; more informal speech is sometimes appropriate. But if teachers decide to use informal speech, they should be aware that they are doing so and make their students aware of the difference. Teachers' language should also reflect a careful choice of words and a vocabulary suitable to the richness of a discipline.

Documentation

Information about the clarity and accuracy of teacher communication is derived primarily from classroom observation.

Figure 6.12

DOMAIN 3: INSTRUCTION
Component 3a: Communicating Clearly and Accurately
Elements:
Directions and procedures • Oral and written language

ELEMENT	LEVEL OF PERFORMANCE			
	UNSATISFACTORY	BASIC	PROFICIENT	DISTINGUISHED
Directions and Procedures	Teacher directions and procedures are confusing to students.	Teacher directions and procedures are clarified after initial student confusion or are excessively detailed.	Teacher directions and procedures are clear to students and contain an appropriate level of detail.	Teacher directions and procedures are clear to students and anticipate possible student misunderstanding.
Oral and Written Language	Teacher's spoken language is inaudible, or written language is illegible. Spoken or written language may contain many grammar and syntax errors. Vocabulary may be inappropriate, vague, or used incorrectly, leaving students confused.	Teacher's spoken language is audible, and written language is legible. Both are used correctly. Vocabulary is correct but limited or is not appropriate to students' ages or backgrounds.	Teacher's spoken and written language is clear and correct. Vocabulary is appropriate to students' age and interests.	Teacher's spoken and written language is correct and expressive, with well-chosen vocabulary that enriches the lesson.

DOMAIN 3: INSTRUCTION

COMPONENT 3b: USING QUESTIONING AND DISCUSSION TECHNIQUES

Rationale and Explanation

Teachers' skill in questioning and in leading discussions is valuable for many instructional purposes, eliciting student reflection and challenging deeper student engagement.

Before teachers have acquired skill in questioning and discussion, they tend to pose primarily rapid-fire, short-answer, low-level questions to their students, using the questions as a vehicle for students to demonstrate their knowledge. Such questioning is better labeled "recitation" than "discussion," because the questions are not true questions but rather a form of quiz in which teachers elicit from students their knowledge on a particular topic.

Alternatively, poor questions may be those that are boring, comprehensible to only a few students, or narrow—the teacher has a single answer in mind even when choices are possible.

When teachers use skilled questioning, they engage their students in an exploration of content. Carefully framed questions enable students to reflect on their understanding and consider new possibilities. The questions rarely require a simple yes/no response and may have many possible correct answers. Experienced teachers allow students time to think before they must respond to a question and encourage all students to participate. Teachers often probe a student's answer, seeking clarification or elaboration through such questions

as, "Could you give an example of that?" or "Would you explain further what you mean?" Teachers show students how to frame questions of high cognitive challenge and how to use the questions to extend learning.

Experienced teachers also cultivate their skills in leading discussions. As a result, class discussions are animated, engaging all students in important questions and using the discussion format as a technique to extend knowledge. In a well-run discussion, a teacher does not hold the center stage but rather encourages students to comment on one another's answers and request further elaboration. In classes accustomed to discussion, students assume considerable responsibility for the depth and breadth of the discussions.

In a well-run discussion, all students are engaged. The dialogue is not dominated by a few "star" students, and the teacher is not simply waiting for someone to provide the answer he has been looking for. Rather, all students are drawn into the conversation; the perspectives of *all* students are sought; in other words, *all* voices are heard.

One mark of skill in leading discussions is a teacher's response when students pursue an enjoyable but irrelevant tangent. Accomplished teachers are able to pull the group back to the topic, while demonstrating respect for the students.

In a classroom where a teacher uses questions and discussions to enhance learning, the teacher may pose a single, well-crafted question, then wait for a thoughtful response. Follow-up questions like, "Does anyone see another possibility?" or "Who would like to comment on Jerry's idea?" may provide a focus for an entire class period. The teacher gradually moves from the center to the side of the discussion and encourages students to maintain the momentum. At times, the teacher may find it necessary to rephrase the question to refocus group attention on the topic. But in the hands of a skilled teacher, discussion becomes a vehicle for deep exploration of content.

Lastly, a well-run discussion uses questions the students pose. The formulation of questions requires that students engage in analytical thinking and motivates them more than questions the teacher presents.

Documentation

Teachers' skill in questioning and discussion techniques is seen almost exclusively in classroom observation. The initial questions may be included on the Instruction Plan for a Single Lesson (see Chapter 4).

Figure 6.13	**DOMAIN 3: INSTRUCTION** **Component 3b: Using Questioning and Discussion Techniques** *Elements:* *Quality of questions • Discussion techniques • Student participation*

LEVEL OF PERFORMANCE

ELEMENT	UNSATISFACTORY	BASIC	PROFICIENT	DISTINGUISHED
Quality of Questions	Teacher's questions are virtually all of poor quality.	Teacher's questions are a combination of low and high quality. Only some invite a response.	Most of teacher's questions are of high quality. Adequate time is available for students to respond.	Teacher's questions are of uniformly high quality, with adequate time for students to respond. Students formulate many questions.
Discussion Techniques	Interaction between teacher and students is predominantly recitation style, with teacher mediating all questions and answers.	Teacher makes some attempt to engage students in a true discussion, with uneven results.	Classroom interaction represents true discussion, with teacher stepping, when appropriate, to the side.	Students assume considerable responsibility for the success of the discussion, initiating topics and making unsolicited contributions.
Student Participation	Only a few students participate in the discussion.	Teacher attempts to engage all students in the discussion, but with only limited success.	Teachers successfully engages all students in the discussion.	Students themselves ensure that all voices are heard in the discussion.

DOMAIN 3: INSTRUCTION

COMPONENT 3C:
ENGAGING STUDENTS IN LEARNING

Rationale and Explanation

If one component can claim to be the most important, this is the one. Engaging students in learning is the raison d'être of education. All other components are in the service of student engagement, from planning and preparation, to establishing a supportive environment, to reflecting on classroom events. Lack of engagement is easy to spot, manifesting itself as students doodling on their notebooks, passing notes, or gazing out the window. Occasionally, lack of engagement takes more aggressive forms, such as disruptive students.

Student engagement is not the same as "time on task," a concept that refers to student involvement in instructional activities. Students may be completing a worksheet (rather than talking or passing notes) and therefore "on task," even if the worksheet does not engage them in significant learning. Perhaps the worksheet requires skills and knowledge that they do not yet have, or it represents concepts that because the students learned them long ago, constitute no challenge. Mere activity, then, is inadequate for engagement. Nor is simple participation sufficient. What is required for student engagement is *intellectual involvement* with the content, or active construction of understanding. School, in other words, is not a spectator sport.

Successful instruction requires the active and invested participation of all parties.

Physical materials may enhance student engagement in learning. For example, many elementary-level mathematics concepts are best explained and explored through using physical representations. When students use physical materials, they are more likely to be actively engaged in learning than if they don't use them. But physical materials are no guarantee of engagement—students can mess around unproductively with manipulatives, learning nothing. What is required is *mental engagement,* which may or may not involve physical activity. Hands-on activity is not enough; it must also be "minds-on."

Students can be engaged in different ways, making mental engagement more difficult to identify. For example, suppose a teacher is introducing the concept of symbolism in literature or explaining the difference between active and passive solar energy. The method for presenting information may be reading, followed by small-group discussion or a teacher-led minipresentation, followed by an individual activity. If the instructional goals relate to thinking and reasoning skills (e.g., the collection and analysis of data), the preferred approach may be independent student investigations, conducted either individually or in small groups. Even if the instructional goals relate to information that must eventually be learned by rote (e.g., multiplication facts), the activities can still engage students intellectually, such as searching for patterns in the numbers or devising techniques to enhance memorization.

Student engagement consists of several distinct, though related, elements.

• **Representation of Content.** All teachers face the challenge of helping students understand new content. The new content may consist of concepts (e.g., buoyancy and density or place value), skills (e.g., a basketball layup), or relationships (e.g., role of the Renaissance on the development of art in Europe). How this content is presented, or represented, to students has enormous bearing on their understanding. When students remember a teacher years afterward, it is often the teacher's skill in this area that has been memorable.

Skilled teachers select examples and metaphors that illuminate the new ideas or skills, connecting new content to students' knowledge, interests, and a school's culture. For example, in explaining the Trojan Horse, a teacher may liken it to a possible (or actual) infiltration of a high school's football team by the opposition. Presentation of content can take the form of oral description, visual representation (through some type of graphic organizer), or teacher-led discussion.

• **Activities and Assignments** (including homework). For students to engage deeply with content, they must participate in learning activities that challenge them to construct understanding. These activities and assignments may take many forms and depend on the context, but they tend to share certain characteristics:

◊ *Emphasize problem-based learning.* Many successful, constructivist activities and assignments require that students solve a problem or answer an important question. For example, when 4th graders determine which set of objects conducts electricity, or when high school students determine if the number of delegates to the Constitutional Convention was related to each state's population, they are engaging in problem solving. That each question actually has a correct answer does not make it trivial. The students must determine an approach, interpret their findings, and possibly formulate additional questions. From their point of view, they are answering a question and engaging in problem-based learning.

◊ *Permit student choice and initiative.* Many well-designed activities encourage or even require students to make choices and take initiative. To some degree, student choice naturally accompanies a problem-based approach. But in addition, even when activities and assignments are not problem based (e.g., a journal entry), students are more deeply engaged in the content if they have a high degree of choice on the details of the activity. The highest level of student engagement is when students exercise initiative in formulating their own questions and designing their own investigations.

◊ *Encourage depth rather than breadth.* Activities and assignments designed to enhance student engagement are not superficial. They challenge students to search for underlying causes, explain their thinking, and justify a position. Work designed for depth represents an appropriate cognitive challenge for students, not permitting easy answers or flippant responses. Typically, such activities engage students in generating knowledge, finding patterns, and testing hypotheses.

◊ *Require student thinking.* Activities and assignments that students can complete without thinking are not engaging them. Of course, the level of thinking required must be appropriate to students' age and skill. What is considered a trivial bit of knowledge for an adult (such as identifying the different ways to make 23 cents with coins) represents high-level thinking for 1st graders. The optimal level of thinking needed for a task stretches students—but they can still complete it successfully. Ensuring this success for large numbers of diverse students is not an easy task, which is why activities and assignments that can be approached on several levels are particularly suitable for a diverse group.

◊ *Designed to be relevant and authentic.* Typically, activities and assignments designed for maximum student engagement represent relevant and authentic applications of knowledge. Searching for a contemporary analogy or metaphor for a historical event is an effective technique to promote deep understanding. Some content, however, is and must be abstract, such as the behavior of trigonometric functions.

• **Grouping of Students.** Students may be grouped in many different ways to enhance their level of engagement: in a single, large group, led by either the teacher or another student; in small groups, either independently or in an instructional setting with a teacher; and independently. In small groups, the ability level and skill in an area can be homogeneous or heterogeneous. Students can choose their own grouping, with partners, in triads, or in other configurations that they or a teacher establish.

Teacher decisions about student grouping are based on a number of considerations. Chief among these is suitability to the instructional goals. Most important, the type of instructional group should reflect what a teacher is trying to accomplish and should serve those purposes.

• **Use of Instructional Materials and Resources.** Instructional materials can include any items that assist students in engaging with content: textbooks, readings, lab equipment, maps, charts, films, videos, and math manipulatives. Instructional materials are not, in themselves, engaging or unengaging; rather, it is a teacher's and students' use of the materials that is the determinant. For instance, students can use laboratory materials to formulate and test hypotheses about a phenomenon, or a teacher can use them to present an experiment, with students as simply observers.

• **Structure and Pacing.** Pacing in the classroom is appropriate to the students and content, and suitable opportunities for closure are provided. Students do not feel rushed in their work; nor does time drag while some students are completing their work.

Last, and related to timing, is lesson structure. A well-designed lesson has a defined structure, and students know where they are in that structure. Some lessons have a recognizable beginning, middle, and end, with a clear introduction and closure. Others consist more of a working session, for example, in an art studio. In either case, there is a structure to what happens, and that structure has been created through the teacher's design.

Documentation

Observing a class is the best method for witnessing a teacher's skill in promoting engagement. Other indications include an Instructional Artifact Sheet (see Chapter 4) in a teacher's portfolio, a videotape of a class, and examples of student work.

Figure 6.14

DOMAIN 3: INSTRUCTION
Component 3c: Engaging Students in Learning
Elements:
Representation of content • Activities and assignments • Grouping of students
Instructional materials and resources • Structure and pacing

LEVEL OF PERFORMANCE

ELEMENT	UNSATISFACTORY	BASIC	PROFICIENT	DISTINGUISHED
Representation of Content	Representation of content is inappropriate and unclear or uses poor examples and analogies.	Representation of content is inconsistent in quality: Some is done skillfully, with good examples; other portions are difficult to follow.	Representation of content is appropriate and links well with students' knowledge and experience.	Representation of content is appropriate and links well with students' knowledge and experience. Students contribute to representation of content.
Activities and Assignments	Activities and assignments are inappropriate for students in terms of their age or backgrounds. Students are not engaged mentally.	Some activities and assignments are appropriate to students and engage them mentally, but others do not.	Most activities and assignments are appropriate to students. Almost all students are cognitively engaged in them.	All students are cognitively engaged in the activities and assignments in their exploration of content. Students initiate or adapt activities and projects to enhance understanding.
Grouping of Students	Instructional groups are inappropriate to the students or to the instructional goals.	Instructional groups are only partially appropriate to the students or only moderately successful in advancing the instructional goals of a lesson.	Instructional groups are productive and fully appropriate to the students or to the instructional goals of a lesson.	Instructional groups are productive and fully appropriate to the instructional goals of a lesson. Students take the initiative to influence instructional groups to advance their understanding.

Figure 6.14—continued

DOMAIN 3: INSTRUCTION
Component 3c: Engaging Students in Learning
Elements:
Representation of content • Activities and assignments • Grouping of students
Instructional materials and resources • Structure and pacing

ELEMENT	LEVEL OF PERFORMANCE			
	UNSATISFACTORY	BASIC	PROFICIENT	DISTINGUISHED
Instructional Materials and Resources	Instructional materials and resources are unsuitable to the instructional goals or do not engage students mentally.	Instructional materials and resources are partially suitable to the instructional goals, or students' level of mental engagement is moderate.	Instructional materials and resources are suitable to the instructional goals and engage students mentally.	Instructional materials and resources are suitable to the instructional goals and engage students mentally. Students initiate the choice, adaptation, or creation of materials to enhance their own purposes.
Structure and Pacing	The lesson has no clearly defined structure, or the pacing of the lesson is too slow or rushed, or both.	The lesson has a recognizable structure, although it is not uniformly maintained throughout the lesson. Pacing of the lesson is inconsistent.	The lesson has a clearly defined structure around which the activities are organized. Pacing of the lesson is consistent.	The lesson's structure is highly coherent, allowing for reflection and closure as appropriate. Pacing of the lesson is appropriate for all students.

DOMAIN 3: INSTRUCTION

COMPONENT 3d:
PROVIDING FEEDBACK TO STUDENTS

Rationale and Explanation

Feedback is information teachers provide to students about their progress in learning. In using feedback, such as comments on a piece of writing or an explanation of how the process a student used in a math problem was misguided, students advance their understanding. The process of feedback individualizes instruction. Even when instructional goals and learning activities are common to an entire class, the experience of individual students is distinct.

It is essential that teachers provide feedback equitably, that *all* students receive feedback on their work. It is not equitable, for example, for a few star pupils to receive detailed and constructive suggestions on their papers, while others receive negative feedback only, or the teacher gives little attention to other students' work.

To provide feedback, teachers must carefully watch and listen to students, who reveal their level of understanding through the questions they ask, their approaches to projects and assignments, and the work they produce. Students frequently surprise their teachers with their interests and insights. Based on such unexpected events, teachers occasionally alter their plans so that students can pursue alternate instructional goals from those originally envisioned.

Teachers typically provide feedback to students on their learning—perhaps subtly, such as a quizzical look as a student attempts an explanation or nods of encouragement as a student works through a math problem. But there are other sources in addition to teachers:

- Instructional activities, for example, when students discover from a science experiment that their understanding was incorrect.
- Materials, for example, the answers to math problems in the back of a textbook.
- Computer programs.
- Other students, for example, peer review of a writing assignment.

Feedback should be provided on all significant work: papers, tests, quizzes, and classwork. Some student assignments are valuable even if students receive no feedback. An example is student improvement in writing fluency through simply writing. But most student learning depends on attention to instructional goals, with teachers assisting on meeting those goals. This focus implies that opportunities for feedback should be fully exploited by means such as written comments on a student's test, a teacher-student conference, or teacher feedback using an audiotape. Some feedback may be nonverbal. Teachers convey meaning in many ways, from smiles and nods, to a puzzled look, to a reassuring gesture.

To be effective, feedback should be accurate, constructive, substantive, specific, and timely. Global comments such as "very good" do not qualify as feedback, nor do comments to an entire class about the weaknesses of a few students. Peer suggestions may not be accurate or helpful; feedback that undercuts a student's sense of value does not promote learning. A teacher's responsibility is to see that the feedback is accurate. Papers returned three weeks after students handed them in—regardless of the quality of the comments—do not provide timely feedback.

The value of feedback is maximized if students use it in their learning. That is, if students don't use a teacher's comments, they can't learn from them. In most cases, such student use of feedback requires planning by the teacher, and time must be made available for it.

Documentation

Feedback can occasionally be witnessed during a classroom observation, depending on the activities planned for a lesson. But, generally, feedback is documented in other ways, such as in a teacher portfolio containing examples of student work with teacher or peer comments. The timeliness of feedback can also be revealed through student responses to a questionnaire, particularly at the secondary level.

Figure 6.15

DOMAIN 3: INSTRUCTION
Component 3d: Providing Feedback to Students
Elements:
Quality: accurate, substantive, constructive, and specific • Timeliness

ELEMENT	LEVEL OF PERFORMANCE			
	UNSATISFACTORY	BASIC	PROFICIENT	DISTINGUISHED
Quality: Accurate, Substantive, Constructive, and Specific	Feedback is either not provided or is of uniformly poor quality.	Feedback is inconsistent in quality: Some elements of high quality are present; others are not.	Feedback is consistently high quality.	Feedback is consistently high quality. Provision is made for students to use feedback in their learning.
Timeliness	Feedback is not provided in a timely manner.	Timeliness of feedback is inconsistent.	Feedback is consistently provided in a timely manner.	Feedback is consistently provided in a timely manner. Students make prompt use of the feedback in their learning.

DOMAIN 3: INSTRUCTION

COMPONENT 3e: DEMONSTRATING FLEXIBILITY AND RESPONSIVENESS

Rationale and Explanation

Teaching means making hundreds of decisions daily. Some are small and trivial; most are not. The most difficult decisions have to do with adjusting a lesson plan in midstream, when it is apparent that such adjustments will improve students' experience. For example, an activity may be confusing to students or require understanding they have not yet acquired. Alternatively, a planned activity may be suitable for only some students in a class, requiring adjustments for others.

Teachers can demonstrate flexibility and responsiveness in three types of situations. One is an instructional activity that is not working. If students have never heard of a phenomenon on which a teacher is basing an entire explanation, or if an activity is not appropriate for them, the teacher may choose to abandon an entire activity or to modify it significantly. Sometimes, such adjustments involve a major change. At other times, the shift is more modest. Occasionally a change in pace is all that is required; students are lethargic when a pace is too slow, but they become reengaged when the pace picks up.

The second situation that happens occasionally is a spontaneous event that provides an opportunity for valuable learning. A 2nd grader arrives at school with a caterpillar that immediately captures the interest of the entire class. Events at the secondary level, such as an athletic contest or a schoolwide conflict, can divert the attention of the entire school. Handling such events is a challenge every teacher faces, offering a "teachable moment" and a springboard for an important and memorable intellectual experience. Teachers demonstrate flexibility when they seize upon a major event and adapt their lesson to it, fulfilling their instructional goals but in a way that is different from what they had originally planned.

The third manifestation of flexibility and responsiveness relates to a teacher's sense of efficacy and commitment to the learning of all students. When some students experience difficulty in learning, a teacher who is responsive and flexible persists in the search for alternative approaches, not blaming the students, the home environment, or the larger culture for the deficiency.

In general, flexibility and responsiveness are the mark of experience. Novice teachers rarely have the instructional repertoire or the confidence to abandon a lesson plan in midstream and embark in a new direction. Such a response requires both courage and confidence, which come with experience.

Teachers demonstrate lack of flexibility and responsiveness when they stick to a plan, even when the plan is clearly not working; when they brush aside a student's comment or question; or when they quickly dismiss the caterpillar in the interests of returning to "real work." Or teachers may stay with an approach even when it is clearly inappropriate for some students. Such decisions are, indeed, tricky. Sometimes the instructional goals of the day simply cannot accommodate the caterpillar, and the students are not really that interested. But when the conditions are right, flexibility can enrich students' experience. Not every episode in a classroom represents a spontaneous opportunity for learning. But many do, and with experience, teachers become more skilled at exploiting them while still achieving their instructional goals.

Documentation

Flexibility and responsiveness can be observed when they occur in a classroom. A teacher may describe such an event, but it is best observed. There are many lessons in which no such opportunities arise. Their absence is not necessarily a sign of rigidity; rather, it may simply reflect a lack of opportunity.

Figure 6.16

DOMAIN 3: INSTRUCTION
Component 3e: Demonstrating Flexibility and Responsiveness
Elements:
Lesson adjustment • Response to students • Persistence

	LEVEL OF PERFORMANCE			
ELEMENT	UNSATISFACTORY	BASIC	PROFICIENT	DISTINGUISHED
Lesson Adjustment	Teacher adheres rigidly to an instructional plan, even when a change will clearly improve a lesson.	Teacher attempts to adjust a lesson, with mixed results.	Teacher makes a minor adjustment to a lesson, and the adjustment occurs smoothly.	Teacher successfully makes a major adjustment to a lesson.
Response to Students	Teacher ignores or brushes aside students' questions or interests.	Teacher attempts to accommodate students' questions or interests. The effects on the coherence of a lesson are uneven.	Teacher successfully accommodates students' questions or interests.	Teacher seizes a major opportunity to enhance learning, building on a spontaneous event.
Persistence	When a student has difficulty learning, the teacher either gives up or blames the student or the environment for the student's lack of success.	Teacher accepts responsibility for the success of all students but has only a limited repertoire of instructional strategies to use.	Teacher persists in seeking approaches for students who have difficulty learning, possessing a moderate repertoire of strategies.	Teacher persists in seeking effective approaches for students who need help, using an extensive repertoire of strategies and soliciting additional resources from the school.

DOMAIN 4: PROFESSIONAL RESPONSIBILITIES

COMPONENT 4a: REFLECTING ON TEACHING

Rationale and Explanation

Many educators, as well as researchers, believe that the ability to reflect on teaching is the mark of a true professional. Through reflection, real growth and therefore excellence are possible. By trying to understand the consequences of actions and by contemplating alternative courses of action, teachers expand their repertoire of practice.

Reflection on teaching includes the thinking that follows any instructional event. During that follow-up thinking, teachers consider if their goals were met and if a lesson "worked." Sensitivity to the engagement of students—both in quantity and quality—helps teachers know to what extent the approach used was appropriate or if an alternative approach would have been more effective. Of course, judgments on effectiveness are related to the quality of subsequent student participation and students' success on assessments, which may not be known for several days.

Beginning teachers need to cultivate the skill of accurate reflection. Novices tend to believe that a lesson was "fine" if the students were busy throughout the lesson and if they themselves survived the effort. With experience, teachers become more discerning and can evaluate their successes as well as their errors. Accuracy in these judgments helps teachers refine their approach the next time, plus improve their practice. This constant improvement is the true benefit of reflection, enabling teachers to focus on those aspects of their teaching that can be strengthened.

In addition to making accurate judgments, teachers must use these reflections in practice. Most teachers have an opportunity to teach the same topic another year, or even the next class period. By reflecting on what went well and what could have been strengthened, teachers are able to improve their next encounter with a topic. And since many of the principles they learn from reflecting on practice apply to many instructional settings, their overall teaching generally improves.

Documentation

Teachers demonstrate their skill in reflection through completing the Reflection Sheet (see Chapter 4). They may also demonstrate their insights through professional conversation with colleagues.

Figure 6.17

DOMAIN 4: PROFESSIONAL RESPONSIBILITIES
Component 4a: Reflecting on Teaching
Elements:
Accuracy • Use in future teaching

	L E V E L O F P E R F O R M A N C E			
ELEMENT	UNSATISFACTORY	BASIC	PROFICIENT	DISTINGUISHED
Accuracy	Teacher does not know if a lesson was effective or achieved its goals, or profoundly misjudges the success of a lesson.	Teacher has a generally accurate impression of a lesson's effectiveness and the extent to which instructional goals were met.	Teacher makes an accurate assessment of a lesson's effectiveness and the extent to which it achieved its goals and can cite general references to support the judgment.	Teacher makes a thoughtful and accurate assessment of a lesson's effectiveness and the extent to which it achieved its goals, citing many specific examples from the lesson and weighing the relative strength of each.
Use in Future Teaching	Teacher has no suggestions for how a lesson may be improved another time.	Teacher makes general suggestions about how a lesson may be improved.	Teacher makes a few specific suggestions of what he may try another time.	Drawing on an extensive repertoire of skills, the teacher offers specific alternative actions, complete with probable successes of different approaches.

DOMAIN 4: PROFESSIONAL RESPONSIBILITIES

COMPONENT 4b:
MAINTAINING ACCURATE RECORDS

Rationale and Explanation

One reflection of the complexity of teaching is the need for teachers to keep accurate records. Although not an inherent part of interaction with students, such records inform those interactions and enable teachers to respond to individual needs.

When teachers make assignments, particularly those with important deadlines, they must keep track of which students have completed which assignments, fully or in part. Few shortcomings of teachers are more irritating to students—particularly at the secondary level—than a habit of losing or otherwise not registering student work. A well-designed system for assignments enables both teacher and students to know at all times which assignments have been completed and which are still outstanding.

Teachers must also keep track of student learning so that they know which parts of the curriculum students have learned and which are still awaiting understanding. Such tracking may take the form of skills checklists, records of competencies that are demonstrated, and portfolios of student work. A system for monitoring student progress must align with a teacher's approach to assessment (Component 1f). For example, if performance tasks are used to evaluate student understanding, then the records must include the level of student success on those tasks and provide the information for feedback to students (Component 3d). Similarly, records of student progress enable a teacher to provide information to families (Component 4c).

Records must also be maintained on the noninstructional activities that are essential to a school's smooth operation. For example, records of which students have returned their signed permission slips for a field trip and records of which students regularly buy milk for lunch all need to be kept accurately. Teachers are also required to complete certain paperwork, such as inventories and ordering supplies, in an accurate and timely fashion.

Many successful record-keeping methods are managed as paper-and-pencil systems. In this age of inexpensive computer technology, however, many teachers have discovered that they can maintain better records with electronic assistance.

Documentation

Information showing teachers' skill in maintaining accurate records is derived from portfolio items, such as a grade book, skills worksheets, results of student assessments, and records of classroom noninstructional duties.

Figure 6.18	DOMAIN 4: PROFESSIONAL RESPONSIBILITIES Component 4b: Maintaining Accurate Records *Elements:* *Student completion of assignments • Student progress in learning • Noninstructional records*			

	LEVEL OF PERFORMANCE			
ELEMENT	UNSATISFACTORY	BASIC	PROFICIENT	DISTINGUISHED
Student Completion of Assignments	Teacher's system for maintaining information on student completion of assignments is in disarray.	Teacher's system for maintaining information on student completion of assignments is rudimentary and only partially effective.	Teacher's system for maintaining information on student completion of assignments is fully effective.	Teacher's system for maintaining information on student completion of assignments is fully effective. Students participate in the maintenance of records.
Student Progress in Learning	Teacher has no system for maintaining information on student progress in learning, or the system is in disarray.	Teacher's system for maintaining information on student progress in learning is rudimentary and partially effective.	Teacher's system for maintaining information on student progress in learning is effective.	Teacher's system for maintaining information on student progress in learning is fully effective. Students contribute information and interpretation of the records.
Noninstruc- tional Records	Teacher's records for noninstructional activities are in disarray, resulting in errors and confusion.	Teacher's records for noninstructional activities are adequate, but they require frequent monitoring to avoid error.	Teacher's system for maintaining information on noninstructional activities is fully effective.	Teacher's system for maintaining information on noninstructional activities is highly effective, and students contribute to its maintenance.

DOMAIN 4: PROFESSIONAL RESPONSIBILITIES

COMPONENT 4C:
COMMUNICATING WITH FAMILIES

Rationale and Explanation

As the African proverb reminds us, "It takes a village to raise a child." Educators have long recognized that when they can enlist the participation of students' families in the educational process, student learning is enhanced. Although parents and guardians vary enormously in how active a part they can take in their children's learning, most parents care deeply about the progress of their children and appreciate meaningful participation. The relationship between parents and teachers also depends on the age of the children; most kindergarten teachers have far greater contact with the families of their students than do high school teachers.

Communication with families involves keeping them informed of events in a class, such as procedures and grading systems. Such activities are especially important when teachers use approaches that may be unfamiliar to parents. Many vehicles are useful for such communication. Most schools schedule a "back-to-school" night early in the school year for teachers to touch base with parents and explain the goals for the year. Some teachers find that engaging parents in a typical (but brief) instructional activity during that time, particularly if the methods are unfamiliar, is helpful. Teachers may send home a regular newsletter or periodic information on upcoming school and classroom events.

In some communities, parents—possibly because of their own negative school experiences—are reluctant to come to the school. Overcoming this reluctance often requires a deliberate outreach, carried out with sensitivity and goodwill.

In addition, teachers must keep parents informed about the academic and social progress of their children. Schools have formalized procedures for reporting to parents, and many teachers supplement these systems with additional information. Although sometimes difficult to achieve, communicating honestly with parents about their children's learning is essential for teachers. No one is well served when a teacher, however well intentioned, conveys to a parent that a student is "doing fine" when in fact the student is struggling.

When parents express specific concerns about their children in school, it is because they care deeply about their child's progress. Any response should be handled with empathy and respect. Communication with families about individual students must be two-way and occur at times of success as well as when a student is experiencing difficulty.

Many teachers find ways to engage parents in the actual instructional program. Even though this area of communicating with families varies with the age of the students and the subjects taught, much communication is possible. For example, primary grade teachers can send home books that are suitable for bedtime reading or suggestions of activities for parents to do with their children. Older students can be asked to interview an older relative. Most teachers find that when they can engage the families in the actual learning process, all areas of communication are improved.

Documentation

The Family Contact Log (see Chapter 4) provides information about contacts with families of students. Teachers may also add other materials—such as a class newsletter—to their professional portfolio.

Figure 6.19	**DOMAIN 4: PROFESSIONAL RESPONSIBILITIES**

Component 4c: Communicating with Families

Elements:

Information about the instructional program • Information about individual students
Engagement of families in the instructional program

LEVEL OF PERFORMANCE

ELEMENT	UNSATISFACTORY	BASIC	PROFICIENT	DISTINGUISHED
Information About the Instructional Program	Teacher provides little information about the instructional program to families.	Teacher participates in the school's activities for parent communication but offers little additional information.	Teacher provides frequent information to parents, as appropriate, about the instructional program.	Teacher provides frequent information to parents, as appropriate, about the instructional program. Students participate in preparing materials for their families.
Information About Individual Students	Teacher provides minimal information to parents and does not respond or responds insensitively to parent concerns about students.	Teacher adheres to the school's required procedures for communicating to parents. Responses to parent concerns are minimal.	Teacher communicates with parents about students' progress on a regular basis and is available as needed to respond to parent concerns.	Teacher provides information to parents frequently on both positive and negative aspects of student progress. Response to parent concerns is handled with great sensitivity.
Engagement of Families in the Instructional Program	Teacher makes no attempt to engage families in the instructional program, or such attempts are inappropriate.	Teacher makes modest and inconsistently successful attempts to engage families in the instructional program.	Teacher's efforts to engage families in the instructional program are frequent and successful.	Teacher's efforts to engage families in the instructional program are frequent and successful. Students contribute ideas for projects that will be enhanced by family participation.

DOMAIN 4: PROFESSIONAL RESPONSIBILITIES

COMPONENT 4d:
CONTRIBUTING TO THE SCHOOL AND DISTRICT

Rationale and Explanation

Most teachers' duties extend beyond their classroom doors. Educators, either by contractual agreement or by a sense of professional responsibility, find that their days contain such activities as committee meetings, rehearsals for the school play, and assistance with family math night. These individuals have extensive and highly professional relationships with their colleagues, and the fabric of the school is one of mutual support and enhancement.

Relationships with colleagues are an important element of teachers' contribution to the school and district. Professional educators are generous with their expertise and willingly share materials and insights, particularly with those less experienced than they. They are supportive and do not try to score points in a faculty meeting at the expense of other teachers or attempt to manipulate the outcome of a discussion for their own convenience. The focus of their work is the well-being of students, and they collaborate with colleagues to that end. For example, they participate in joint planning of thematic units or coordinate the learning experiences for students with special needs.

Professional educators make many contributions to the life of a school. They assume their share of the duties that help the school function smoothly, whether participating in the PTA, hosting a faculty party, or managing a spelling bee. In some schools, certain additional jobs earn supplementary compensation; in others, the faculty's responsibility, working as a team, is to divide up the jobs. In almost all schools, many opportunities exist for educators to assume additional responsibilities, thereby enhancing the culture of the entire school.

Schools and districts may undertake major projects that require teacher participation. These include site councils, curriculum committees, and study groups with beginning teachers. Such projects, whether they involve serving on the discipline committee or designing new performance assessments, require a considerable investment of time—professional educators find the time.

Documentation

The School and District Contribution Log (see Chapter 4) provides an opportunity for teachers to record their activities in this area.

Figure 6.20

DOMAIN 4: PROFESSIONAL RESPONSIBILITIES
Component 4d: Contributing to the School and District
Elements:
Relationships with colleagues • Service to the school • Participation in school and district projects

	LEVEL OF PERFORMANCE			
ELEMENT	UNSATISFACTORY	BASIC	PROFICIENT	DISTINGUISHED
Relationships with Colleagues	Teacher's relationships with colleagues are negative or self-serving.	Teacher maintains cordial relationships with colleagues to fulfill the duties that the school or district requires.	Support and cooperation characterize relationships with colleagues.	Support and cooperation characterize relationships with colleagues. Teacher takes initiative in assuming leadership among the faculty.
Service to the School	Teacher avoids becoming involved in school events.	Teacher participates in school events when specifically asked.	Teacher volunteers to participate in school events, making a substantial contribution.	Teacher volunteers to participate in school events, making a substantial contribution, and assumes a leadership role in at least some aspect of school life.
Participation in School and District Projects	Teacher avoids becoming involved in school and district projects.	Teacher participates in school and district projects when specifically asked.	Teacher volunteers to participate in school and district projects, making a substantial contribution.	Teacher volunteers to participate in school and district projects, making a substantial contribution, and assumes a leadership role in a major school or district project.

DOMAIN 4: PROFESSIONAL RESPONSIBILITIES

COMPONENT 4e:
GROWING AND DEVELOPING PROFESSIONALLY

Rationale and Explanation

Continuing development is the mark of a true professional, an ongoing effort that is never completed. Educators committed to attaining and remaining at the top of their profession invest much energy in staying informed and increasing their skills. They are then in a position to exercise leadership among colleagues.

Content knowledge is one area where educators can grow and develop professionally. Superficial content knowledge is insufficient for good teaching; deeper understanding is essential. Elementary teachers who provide instruction in all the disciplines face a challenge in understanding them well enough to be a resource to students. Teachers at the secondary level must be experts in their disciplines so they can enable their students to engage with a subject. All teachers can profit from learning more about the subjects they teach. One of the characteristics of the late 20th century has been the rapid expansion of knowledge; many subjects that teachers teach have changed considerably from what they themselves learned in college. Continuing education is needed to stay abreast of the latest developments.

Developments in pedagogy create opportunities for educators to continually improve their practice. Educational research discovers new methods to engage students in learning. Developments in related fields, for example, business management and cultural studies, can suggest promising approaches and applications. Most teachers can profit from a focus on the latest work in pedagogical research and its applications to classroom practice.

Expanding developments in information technology are yet another vehicle for intense professional development. With CD-ROM becoming more commonplace, increasing numbers of schools wired to the Internet, improving quality in software, and more computers labs becoming available, many teachers find they need to keep learning, too.

Professional organizations are an important vehicle for informing educators. Journals written in the language of the practitioner are valuable resources. And conferences, particularly regional ones, are within the reach of most communities. Local universities and state agencies are other valuable resources. All these organizations recognize the complexity of teaching and are committed to assisting practitioners to be as effective as possible.

Many educators find ways to make a substantial contribution to the profession:

• Conducting research in their classrooms and making the results known to their colleagues through conference presentations or articles.

• Supervising student teachers and meeting periodically with the student teacher supervisors.

• Participating or taking a leadership role in study groups with their colleagues.

Documentation

The Professional Development Log and the Professional Contribution Log (see Chapter 4) can be used to document participation in professional activities.

Figure 6.21	**DOMAIN 4: PROFESSIONAL RESPONSIBILITIES**

Component 4e: Growing and Developing Professionally

Elements:
Enhancement of content knowledge and pedagogical skill • Service to the profession

	LEVEL OF PERFORMANCE			
ELEMENT	UNSATISFACTORY	BASIC	PROFICIENT	DISTINGUISHED
Enhancement of Content Knowledge and Pedagogical Skill	Teacher engages in no professional development activities to enhance knowledge or skill.	Teacher participates in professional activities to a limited extent when they are convenient.	Teacher seeks out opportunities for professional development to enhance content knowledge and pedagogical skill.	Teacher seeks out opportunities for professional development and makes a systematic attempt to conduct action research in his classroom.
Service to the Profession	Teacher makes no effort to share knowledge with others or to assume professional responsibilities.	Teacher finds limited ways to contribute to the profession.	Teacher participates actively in assisting other educators.	Teacher initiates important activities to contribute to the profession, such as mentoring new teachers, writing articles for publication, and making presentations.

DOMAIN 4: PROFESSIONAL RESPONSIBILITIES

COMPONENT 4f: SHOWING PROFESSIONALISM

Rationale and Explanation

"Professionalism" is an elusive concept that permeates all aspects of a teacher's work. In addition to their technical skills in planning and implementing the instructional program, accomplished teachers display certain professional qualities that help them to serve their students and their profession.

First, highly professional teachers care deeply for the well-being of their students and step in on their behalf when needed. They are aware of, and alert to, the signs of physical abuse and drug and alcohol abuse. They may locate a winter coat for a child or discuss a student's future plans with the student and her parents.

Second, educators are advocates for their students, particularly those whom the educational establishment has traditionally underserved. They work diligently for their students' best interests, whether that means convincing a colleague that a student deserves an opportunity or supporting a student's efforts at self-improvement.

At times, advocating for students requires challenging long-held assumptions of students, other faculty, or administration. For example, data suggest that girls perform poorly in mathematics and science because they have been led to believe that those are boys' subjects. Convincing girls and other teachers that girls can do well in those courses may require diligence and patience.

Third, highly professional teachers demonstrate a commitment to professional standards in problem solving and decision making. Professional educators maintain an open mind and are willing to attempt new approaches to old problems, even if in the short run they are inconvenienced. They base their judgments and recommendations on hard information rather than on hearsay and tradition. They strive to use the best data available to support action.

Documentation

Teachers display their professional ethics in daily interactions with students and colleagues.

Figure 6.22

DOMAIN 4: PROFESSIONAL RESPONSIBILITIES
Component 4f: Showing Professionalism
Elements:
Service to students • Advocacy • Decision making

	LEVEL OF PERFORMANCE			
ELEMENT	UNSATISFACTORY	BASIC	PROFICIENT	DISTINGUISHED
Service to Students	Teacher is not alert to students' needs.	Teacher's attempts to serve students are inconsistent.	Teacher is moderately active in serving students.	Teacher is highly proactive in serving students, seeking out resources when necessary.
Advocacy	Teacher contributes to school practices that result in some students being ill served by the school.	Teacher does not knowingly contribute to some students being ill served by the school.	Teacher works within the context of a particular team or department to ensure that all students receive a fair opportunity to succeed.	Teacher makes a particular effort to challenge negative attitudes and helps ensure that all students, particularly those traditionally underserved, are honored in the school.
Decision Making	Teacher makes decisions based on self-serving interests.	Teacher's decisions are based on limited though genuinely professional considerations.	Teacher maintains an open mind and participates in team or departmental decision making.	Teacher takes a leadership role in team or departmental decision making and helps ensure that such decisions are based on the highest professional standards.

APPENDIX: THE RESEARCH FOUNDATION

The framework for professional practice is based on the PRAXIS III criteria developed by Educational Testing Service (ETS) after extensive surveys of the research literature, consultation with expert practitioners and researchers, wide-ranging job analyses, summaries of the demands of state licensing programs, and field work. The components include those aspects of teaching that are expected of experienced as well as beginning teachers. The research foundation for the PRAXIS III criteria is summarized here because it is relevant to this framework for teaching. Many of the findings presented derive from *Development of the Knowledge Base for the PRAXIS III: Classroom Performance Assessments Assessment Criteria* (1994) by Carol Anne Dwyer. This Appendix presents in an abbreviated form some results of the extensive research that ETS conducted and described in detail in that publication.

The knowledge base for the PRAXIS III: Classroom Performance Assessments assessment criteria was derived over an extended period (1987–1993) from three distinct sources: the "wisdom of practice" (Shulman 1987) of experienced teachers, the theory and data developed by educational researchers, and the requirements developed by state teacher licensing authorities. These sources of information are interrelated: Both experienced teachers and state licensing bodies draw on the educational research literature for their findings.

The process of developing the assessment criteria for PRAXIS III: Classroom Performance Assessments was iterative, drawing on extensive research on the tasks of teaching. Such work involved conducting job analyses of elementary, middle, and high school beginning teachers, as well as administrators. ETS staff prepared the surveys, with assistance from the American Association of Colleges for Teacher Education, American Federation of Teachers, National Association of Elementary School Principals, National Association of Secondary School Principals, National Association of State Directors of Teacher Education and Certification, and National Education Association. ETS researchers also conducted an extensive literature search to summarize and synthesize the most reliable findings on effective teaching. Drafts of assessment criteria were reviewed by expert panels and subjected to the rigors of pilot and field testing. And the requirements of state licensing agencies were analyzed for their statements of teaching criteria. From this process emerged the assessment criteria used in ETS's PRAXIS III: Classroom Performance Assessments.

As stated in the Preface, the framework for professional practice derives from the same research base as the criteria for PRAXIS III: Classroom Performance Assessments. The framework for teaching, however, differs from PRAXIS III in two important ways: The

framework is intended to apply to the work of all teachers, not only newly licensed ones; and it is designed to be used in professional conversations that accompany mentoring or peer coaching. The PRAXIS III criteria were developed solely for assessment. Leading practitioners extensively reviewed the framework, which was subjected to the rigors of testing in school situations. It is ultimately the validation of individual users (teachers and supervisors), however, that matters. The framework must resonate with the professional vision that individuals bring to their craft. Only when the components are found to be consistent with the way in which individuals view their work will the components be of value.

The framework divides the complex act of teaching into four broad realms of activity, or domains. Each domain consists of five or six components. Using the four domains as a structure, the rest of the Appendix provides the research supporting the components.

DOMAIN 1: PLANNING AND PREPARATION

The research on planning and preparation for teaching is abundant and clear. Shulman's work (1987) supports Component 1a (demonstrating knowledge of content and pedagogy):

> We expect teachers to understand what they teach
> and, when possible, to understand it in several ways.
> They should understand how a given idea relates to
> other ideas within the same subject area and to ideas
> in other subjects as well (p. 14).

He also illuminates the other components of Domain 1:

> The key to distinguishing the knowledge base of teach-
> ing lies at the intersection of content and pedagogy, in
> the capacity of a teacher to transform the content
> knowledge he or she possesses into forms that are
> pedagogically powerful and yet adaptive to the vari-
> ations in ability and background presented by the stu-
> dents (p. 15).

Many other studies emphasize the central role of content knowledge and pedagogical expertise. Most states require some evidence
of this knowledge as a prerequisite for licensing. The National Board
for Professional Teaching Standards (1991) has as one of the five
main principles that is assessed as part of the certification process
the statement that "teachers know the subjects they teach and how
to teach those subjects to students" (p. 3).

The importance of becoming familiar with and building on students' knowledge and skills (Component 1b) is also the locus of
much research and writing:

> There has been an explosion of research [on students'
> prior knowledge] around children's conceptions of
> mathematics or scientific concepts—of school knowl-
> edge and skills in general. This work strongly demon-
> strates that prior conceptions exert a powerful hold
> and are difficult to alter. Contemporary instructional
> aims include inducing conceptual change as a central
> preoccupation (Sykes and Bird 1992, p. 28).

Sykes and Bird (1992), as well as additional authors, support the
constructivist view of learning (and therefore teaching) that underlies
the framework for professional practice. Many researchers, including
Anderson and Smith (1987), conclude that the earlier view of teaching as infusing knowledge into a vacuum has been supplanted by the
view that teaching involves inducing change in an existing body of
knowledge and belief. Reynolds (1992) sums it up: "Competent teachers create lessons that enable students to connect what they know to
new information" (p. 10). To engage students with new knowledge, it
is essential to know what they understand already of that content:

> Representations [of the subject] need to take into ac-
> count what learners are already likely to know and un-
> derstand about the subject matter as well as the
> experiences and knowledge they bring with them from
> their environment (Floden, Buchmann, and Schwille
> 1987, p. 263).

More recently, an American Psychological Association publication (McCombs 1992) defined learning:

> An individual process of constructing meaning from in-
> formation and experience, filtered through each indi-
> vidual's unique perceptions, thoughts, and feelings.

The importance of clear learning goals (Component 1c) is well
documented in the research literature. Jones (1992) cites many studies (Brophy and Good 1986, Walker 1985) demonstrating the link

between effective teaching and learning and the teacher's formulation of learning goals that are appropriate to the students. The importance of goals has also been studied by Clark and Yinger (1977, 1979); Peterson, Marx, and Clark (1978); Stallings and Kaskowitz (1974); McCutcheon (1980); Yinger (1977); Kauchak and Peterson (1987); Druian and Butler (1987); Hohn (1986); and Natriello (1987). An important element of appropriateness relates to the goals' intellectual rigor. Lowered expectations for some students (frequently minority) may be reflected in a watered-down curriculum that precludes the development of higher-order thinking and skills in analysis (Jones 1992, Irvine 1990, Levin 1987, Moll 1988, Oakes 1986, Stage 1989).

The importance of designing coherent instruction (Component 1e) is well documented in the research literature. For example, students learn more and rate their teachers higher when they can understand how facts, concepts, and principles are interrelated (Smith 1985; Van Patten, Chao, and Reigeluth 1986). Armento (1977) and Smith and Sanders (1981) show that students learn better when instruction is logically sequenced. Designing coherent instruction includes knowing what instructional materials may be used (Component 1d). A number of researchers argue for the link between teacher effectiveness, planning of learning activities, and selection of appropriate materials: Clark and Yinger (1979); Emmer, Sanford, Clements, and Martin (1982); Evertson, Anderson, Anderson, and Brophy (1980); McCutcheon (1980); and Peterson, Marx, and Clark (1978).

Researchers cite the importance of assessing student learning for enhancing achievement. Effective teachers plan for the evaluation of student progress in relation to the stated learning goals (Brophy and Good 1986; Porter and Brophy 1987; Reynolds 1992; Rosenshine 1987; Zigmond, Sansone, Miller, Donahoe, and Kohnke 1986). Teachers are consistent in evaluating students' progress and design the evaluations so that they can be used for feedback to students. Multiple types of assessment (e.g., performance assessments, interviews, and constructed response) provide a more complete and accurate picture of student progress than does any single approach (Cryan 1986).

Domain 2: The Classroom Environment

Research on the development of expertise shows that novice teachers must master at least the rudiments of classroom management before they can become skilled at instruction. That is, attention to routines and procedures, the physical environment, and the establishment of norms and expectations for student behavior are prerequisites to good instruction.

Of course, the relationship is not a simple one. Research supports the need for classroom management, and evidence from both research and informal experience indicates that high student engagement in learning is both a cause and an effect of successful classroom management. The relationship is one of "chicken-and-egg." We do know, however, that effective teachers attend to elements of the classroom environment, creating and maintaining an atmosphere of respect, caring, and commitment to important work.

One aspect of the classroom environment that appears to be fairly independent of the others is the physical environment, captured as Component 2e. Evertson (1989) provides a comprehensive overview of the research supporting the importance of physical factors on student learning and minimizing student misbehavior. Specific studies address such factors as effect on student participation rates, student teacher contacts, time on task, attention, and engagement (e.g., Adams and Biddle 1970; Anderson, Evertson, and Emmer 1979; Brophy 1983; Doyle 1986; Emmer, Evertson, Sanford, Clements, and Worsham 1989). Good and Brophy (1984, 1986) report a positive relation- ship between student engagement in learning and a well-arranged learning environment. Goss and Ingersoll (1981) show that well-arranged classrooms contribute positively to student engagement with learning tasks. Morine-Dershimer (1977) shows that teachers who specifically attend to the physical characteristics of their classrooms have students with higher achievement levels than teachers who do not.

Other elements of the classroom environment appear to be more closely related:

> Rules and procedures [in the classrooms of effective teachers] were concrete, explicit, and functional; that is, they contributed to order and work accomplishment. In addition, items were clearly explained to students, signals were used to indicate when actions were to be carried out or stopped, and time was spent rehearsing procedures (Doyle 1986, p. 410).

Evertson and Harris (1992) emphasize the need to establish routines and procedures and teach them along with expectations for appropriate performance. The need for establishing clear routines and linking them to student behavior (Component 2d) is also documented by Brophy (1987):

> *Routines* are standardized methods of handling particular situations. Many of these are consciously adopted by the teacher and even taught to the students in the form of classroom rules and procedures. By banning certain activities and requiring that other activities be done at certain times or in certain ways, rules and procedures simplify the complexities of life in classrooms for both teachers and students by imposing structures that make events more predictable (italics in original) (pp. 6–7).

A positive link appears to exist between efficient routines and procedures and the time available for learning:

> Research on teaching has established that the key to successful classroom management (and to successful instruction as well) is the teacher's ability to maximize the time that students spend actively engaged in worthwhile academic activities . . . and to minimize the time that they spend waiting for activities to get started, making transitions between activities, sitting with nothing to do, or engaging in misconduct (Brophy 1987, p. 5).

Similar findings are reported in the U.S. Department of Education report *What Works* (1987); Anderson (1986); Emans and Milburn (1989); Emmer, Evertson, and Anderson (1980); Evertson and Emmer (1982); Gage (1978); and Ysseldyke, Christenson, and Thurlow (1987).

An environment of respect and rapport (Component 2a) and a culture for learning (Component 2b) are well established characteristics of effective classrooms:

> Consistent *projection of positive expectations, attributions, and social labels* is important in fostering positive self-concepts and related motives that orient them toward prosocial behavior. In short, students who are consistently treated as if they are well-intentioned individuals who respect themselves and others and desire to act responsibly, morally, and prosocially are more likely to live up to these expectations and acquire these qualities than students who are treated as if they had the opposite qualities (italics in original) (Brophy 1987, pp. 23–24).

The notion that teacher enthusiasm and a positive climate in the classroom are correlated with high student achievement is supported by the work of Keith, Tormatzky, and Pettigrew (1974); Rosenshine (1971); and Walberg, Schiller, and Haertel (1979). Positive morale and interest in the subject matter also appear to be related to the establishment of a rapport with students, which leads to supportive relationships between teachers and students (Fraser 1986; Haertel, Walberg, and Haertel 1981; Moors 1979). Leinhardt (1992) addresses

the cultural and social dimensions of knowledge—it is produced, shared, transformed, and distributed among members of a community. The teacher, as a member of this classroom community, functions as a highly knowledgeable guide whose role is to facilitate the acquisition and expand the amount of information available within this group.

An important element of a culture for learning concerns establishing and communicating high expectations for learning. This is a well-traveled road of educational research, particularly as it relates to achievement levels by students traditionally underserved by the schools. For example, in increasingly diverse classroom settings, teachers' judgments about the academic potential of individual students has a documented effect on their academic behavior (Irvine 1990, Rist 1970, Rosenthal 1973). Similar results are reported in a U.S. Department of Education report (1987), Stallings (1982), Baker (1973), and Krupczak (1972).

DOMAIN 3: INSTRUCTION

Educational research during the late 1980s and early 1990s has emphasized constructivist learning (and therefore teaching) and a renewed interest in "teaching for understanding" and "conceptual learning." Much of the earlier research on effective teaching, however, is still relevant and useful to practitioners. One approach is not superior to the others. Rather, as explained earlier, effective practices are designed to achieve desired results. As educators expand their expectations for student learning to include more conceptual understanding or greater skill in problem solving, then the instructional strategies used must correspondingly change.

Effective teachers communicate clearly about goals, learning expectations, and specific instructions for meeting these goals (Component 3a). Edmonds and Frederickson (1978) report that effective schools serving poor children are characterized by leaders who set clear goals and learning expectations. Brophy and Good (1986) provide a research-based rationale for teachers to help students understand a class's learning expectations and get help to achieve those goals.

The research base for questioning and discussion techniques (Component 3b) and student engagement with learning (Component 3c) suggests that effective teachers use questioning strategies that challenge students at several cognitive levels (Goodwin, Sharp, Cloutier, and Diamond (1983). Ellett's work (1990) states that student involvement is needed:

> In teaching students to think, the teacher deliberately structures and uses teaching methods and learning tasks that *actively involve students* in ample opportunities to develop concepts and skills in generating, structuring, transferring, and restructuring knowledge (italics in original) (p. 47).

Sigel (1990) reviewed the literature in this area and came to a similar conclusion:

> Effective teaching requires clear and precise formulation of questions, waiting an appropriate interval for a

student response, and follow-through using the student's response as a base (p. 85).

Other instructional techniques to enhance student engagement and achievement include frequent review, multiple learning tasks, engaging and appropriate material, and clear explanations that highlight key concepts and make use of appropriate metaphors (Brophy and Good 1986; Conoley 1988; Druian and Butler 1987; Osborn, Jones, and Stein 1985; Reynolds 1992; Rosenshine 1983; Taylor and Valentine 1985; Williams 1988; Zigmond, Sansone, Miller, Donahoe, and Kohnke 1986).

Providing feedback to students on their learning (Component 3d) is well supported in the research literature. A U.S. Department of Education report (1987) includes the need for constructive feedback from teachers, such as praise and specific suggestions, as one characteristic of effective teachers. Rosenshine and Furst (1971) found that students become more proficient at mathematics problem solving when their teachers provide frequent feedback. Similar findings are reported by Sanford and Evertson (1980); Emmer (1982); Carter, Cushing, Sabers, Stein, and Berliner (1988); Porter and Brophy (1987, 1988); and Stallings and Kaskowitz (1974). The National Board for Professional Teaching Standards (1991) identified the concept that "teachers are responsible for managing and monitoring student learning" as one of its five assessment principles for a national board certificate.

Newer research and the "wisdom of practice" (Shulman 1987) recognize the limitations of using standardized tests as the sole measures of achievement. Educators are looking to other research methodologies, focusing less on single lessons and more on case studies of entire units of study, and other success criteria (e.g., more performance assessments and other constructed response formats). This more recent research has discovered (and in some cases rediscovered) the potential for problem- and project-based learning, students asking their own questions and conducting their own investigations, and a teacher's role as facilitator and resource manager (Brandt 1992, 1994; Gardner and Boix-Mansilla 1994; Heckman 1994; Cohen, McLaughlin, and Talbert 1993; Nias, Southworth, and Campbell 1992; Perkins and Blythe 1994; Perrone 1994; Wiske 1994; Wolf 1987; Woods 1994).

This new focus on constructivist learning builds, of course, on earlier work by Dewey and educators committed to implementing the implications of Piaget's work in the classroom. For example, Wolk (1994) cites studies from the early part of the century as a foundation for his work in project-based learning: Hennes (1921) and Kilpatrick (1918, 1925). Current journals are filled with examples of students functioning as researchers engaged in authentic work: The November 1994 issue of *Educational Leadership* ("Strategies for Success") has "strategies for success" as its theme. This new emphasis is a far cry from the focus on skill-based instruction, administered in small steps, and assessed using a norm-referenced, standardized, multiple-choice test.

DOMAIN 4: PROFESSIONAL RESPONSIBILITIES

Educators and researchers have gradually expanded the definition of teaching to include not only classroom interaction between teachers and students but also the full range of responsibilities that comprise teaching. Three of the five key principles that the National Board for Professional Teaching Standards (1991) cite as the foundation for the assessment of accomplished teachers and the awarding of advanced certificates fall into Domain 4:

• "Teachers are committed to students and their learning" (included in Component 4f).
• "Teachers think systematically about their practice and learn from experience" (included in Component 4a).
• "Teachers are members of learning communities" (included in Component 4d).

As teaching becomes increasingly grounded in research, the concept of teaching as a true profession, with all the implications of such a transformation, is becoming more evident.

Teacher professionalism is still a relatively young and evolving field, and the available research reflects this stage. Much of the research is theoretical and grounded in logical and ethical rather than empirical studies, such as the teacher as researcher; the exact dimensions of professional development; the benefits of contributing to the school, district, and the profession; and the nature of professional decision making.

A number of studies do guide practitioners, however, particularly in the areas of teacher reflection, advocacy, collaboration with colleagues, and communication with families. Many studies document the value of teacher reflection, either alone or in collaboration with colleagues, by investigating the reflection on practice by either student teachers or more experienced professionals: Tabachnick and Zeichner (1991); Ross and Regan (1993); Colton and Sparks-Langer (1992, 1993); Ellwein, Graue, and Comfort (1990); Borko, Lalik, and Tomchin (1987); Borko, Livingston, McCaleb, and Mauro (1988); and Borko and Livingston (1989). Other recent studies documenting the value of teacher reflection is found in Calderhead (1989), Grimmett and Erickson (1988), Kemessis (1987), Schön (1987), and Weiss and Louden (1989).

In summarizing a long program of research conducted by the Institute for Research on Teaching, Porter and Brophy (1987, 1988) conclude that effective teachers accept personal responsibility for student learning and behavior. Such teachers engage in corrective, problem-solving approaches with failing students rather than punishing them for their shortcomings. The positive effects of this sense of efficacy is demonstrated in other studies as well—for example, Jones (1992), Smylie (1988), Stein and Wang (1988), Pajares (1992), and Schunk (1991).

The link between teacher collaboration and student achievement has long been recognized. The U.S. Department of Education report *What Works* (1987) states:

> Students benefit academically when their teachers share ideas, cooperate in activities, and assist one

another's intellectual growth . . . . Good instruction flourishes when teachers collaborate (p. 80).

Griffin (1986) characterizes the effective teacher:

> [An effective teacher] interacts with students, colleagues, and community members purposefully and effectively. The individual sees teaching as more than meeting with students and works with peers to identify and act on problems in the classrooms and schools (p. 15).

The link between parent involvement in schools and student learning is well established. Again, the U.S. Department of Education report *What Works* (1987) points to parent involvement as a critical component of effective educational practice. Jones (1992) and Cruickshank (1990) cite the department as suggesting that, in general, student learning is enhanced when teachers work at parent involvement. In particular, sensitive and respectful communication with families of minority children can provide an important avenue for success (Cazden 1986, Hilliard 1989, Irvine 1989, Michaels 1981). More recently, Powell, Casanova, and Berliner (1991) provide an up-to-date review of the research on parent involvement and its effect on student learning. In this set of readings, they establish that parent involvement is intimately associated with academic achievement and that there are a variety of ways for teachers to establish and enhance such involvement.

REFERENCES

Adams, R., and B. Biddle. (1970). *Realities of Teaching: Explorations with Videotape*. New York: Holt, Rinehart, and Winston.

Anderson, C.W., and E.L. Smith. (1987). "Teaching Science." In *The Educator's Handbook: A Research Perspective*, edited by V. Koehler. New York: Longman.

Anderson, L., C.M. Evertson, and E.L. Emmer. (1979). "Dimensions in Classroom Management Derived from Recent Research." In *Perspectives on Classroom Management Research*. Symposium conducted at the annual meeting of the American Educational Research Association. San Francisco. (ERIC Document Reproduction Service No. ED 175 860).

Anderson, L.W. (April 1986). "Research on Teaching and Educational Effectiveness." *National Association of Secondary School Principals Curriculum Report* 15, 4: entire issue. (ERIC Document Reproduction Service No. ED 269 868).

Armento, B. (1977). "Teacher Behaviors Related to Student Achievement on a Social Science Concept Test." *Journal of Teacher Education* 28, 3: 46–52.

Baker, S.H. (1973). "Teacher Effectiveness and Social Class as Factors in Teacher Expectancy Effects on Pupils' Scholastic Achievement." (Doctoral Diss., Clark University). *Dissertation Abstracts International* 34, 2376A.

Borko, H., R. Lalik, and E. Tomchin. (1987). "Student Teachers' Understandings of Successful and Unsuccessful Teaching." *Teaching and Teacher Education* 3, 2: 77–90.

Borko, H., and C. Livingston. (1989). "Cognition and Improvisation: Differences in Mathematics Instruction by Expert and Novice Teachers." *American Educational Research Journal* 26, 4: 473–498.

Borko, H., C. Livingston, J. McCaleb, and L. Mauro. (1988). "Student Teachers' Planning and Post-Lesson Reflections: Patterns and Implications of Teacher Preparation." In *Teachers' Professional Learning*, edited by J. Calderhead. Philadelphia: Falmer Press.

Brandt, R. (1992). "On Research on Teaching: A Conversation with Lee Shulman." *Educational Leadership* 49, 7: 14–19.

Brandt, R. (1994). "On Making Sense: A Conversation with Magdalene Lampert." *Educational Leadership* 51, 5: 26–30.

Brophy, J.E. (1983). "Classroom Organization and Management." *Elementary School Journal* 83, 4: 265–286.

Brophy, J.E. (1987). "Educating Teachers About Managing Classrooms and Students." Occasional Paper No. 115. East Lansing: Institute for Research on Teaching, Michigan State University.

Brophy, J.E., and T.L. Good. (1986). "Teacher Behavior and Student Achievement." In *Handbook of Research on Teaching*, 3rd ed., edited by M.C. Wittrock. New York: Macmillan.

Calderhead, J. (1989). "Reflective Teaching and Teacher Education." *Teaching and Teacher Education* 5, 1: 43–51.

Carnegie Foundation for the Advancement of Teaching. (1987). *A Nation Prepared: Teachers for the 21st Century.* Princeton, N.J.: Author.

Carter, K., K. Cushing, D. Sabers, P. Stein, and D. Berliner. (1988). "Expert-Novice Differences in Perceiving and Processing Visual Classroom Information." *Journal of Teacher Education* 39, 1: 25–31.

Cazden, C. (1986). "Classroom Discourse." In *Handbook of Research on Teaching,* 3rd ed., edited by M.C. Wittrock. New York: Macmillan.

Clark, C.M., and R.J. Yinger. (1977). "Research on Teacher Thinking." *Curriculum Inquiry* 7, 4: 279–304.

Clark, C.M., and R.J. Yinger. (1979). *Three Studies of Teacher Planning.* (Research Series No. 55). East Lansing: Institute for Research on Teaching, Michigan State University.

Cohen, D.K., M.W. McLaughlin, and J.E. Talbert, eds. (1993). *Teaching for Understanding: Challenges for Policy and Practice.* San Francisco: Jossey-Bass.

Colton, A.B., and G.M. Sparks-Langer. (1992). "Restructuring Student Teaching Experiences." In *Supervision in Transition*, edited by C.D. Glickman. Alexandria, Va.: Association for Supervision and Curriculum Development.

Colton, A.B., and G.M. Sparks-Langer. (1993). "A Conceptual Framework to Guide the Development of Teacher Reflection and Decision Making." *Journal of Teacher Education* 44, 1: 45–54.

Conoley, J. (January 1988). "Positive Classroom Ecology." *Bios*, 2–7.

Cruickshank, D.R. (1990). *Research That Informs Teachers and Teacher Educators.* Bloomington, Ind.: Phi Delta Kappa Educational Foundation.

Cryan, J. (1986). "Evaluation: Plague or Promise?" *Childhood Education* 62, 5: 344–350.

Doyle, W. (1986). "Classroom Organization and Management." In *Handbook of Research on Teaching,* 3rd ed., edited by M.C. Wittrock. New York: Macmillan.

Druian, G., and J. Butler. (1987). *School Improvement Research Series. Research You Can Use.* Portland, Oreg.: Northwest Regional Educational Laboratory. (ERIC Document Reproduction Service No. ED 291 145).

Dwyer, C.A. (1994). *Development of the Knowledge Base for the PRAXIS III: Classroom Performance Assessments Assessment Criteria.* Princeton, N.J.: Educational Testing Service.

Dwyer, C.A., and A.M. Villegas. (1993). *Guiding Conceptions and Assessment Principles for the Praxis Series: Professional Assessments for Beginning Teachers.* (Research Report No. 93–17). Princeton, N.J.: Educational Testing Service.

Edmonds, R., and N. Frederickson. (1978). *Search for Effective Schools: The Identification and Analysis of City Schools That Are Instructionally Effective for Poor Children.* Cambridge, Mass.: Harvard University Center for Policy Studies.

Ellett, C. (1990). *A New Generation of Classroom-Based Assessments of Teaching and Learning: Concepts, Issues and Controversies from Pilots of the Louisiana STAR.* Baton Rouge: College of Education, Louisiana State University.

Ellwein, M.C., M.E. Graue, and R.E. Comfort. (1990). "Talking About Instruction: Student Teachers' Reflections on Success and Failure in the Classroom." *Journal of Teacher Education* 41, 4: 3–14.

Emans, R., and C. Milburn. (1989). *The Knowledge Base of Teaching: A Review and Commentary of Process-Product Research.* Vermillion: The University of South Dakota School of Education.

Emmer, E.T. (July 1982). *Management Strategies in Elementary School Classrooms.* (R&D Reproduction Service No. 6052). Austin: The University of Texas at Austin, Research and Development Center for Teacher Education.

Emmer, E.T., C.M. Evertson, and L.M. Anderson. (1980). "Effective Classroom Management at the Beginning of the School Year." *The Elementary School Journal* 80, 5: 219–231.

Emmer, E.T., C.M. Evertson, J.P. Sanford, B.S. Clements, and M.E. Worsham. (1989). *Classroom Management for Secondary Teachers,* 2nd ed. Englewood Cliffs, N.J.: Prentice-Hall.

Emmer, E.T., J.P. Sanford, B.S. Clements, and J. Martin. (1982). *Improving Classroom Management and Organization in Junior High Schools: An Experiential Investigation.* (R&D Report No. 6153). Austin: The University of Texas at Austin, Research and Development Center for Teacher Education.

Evertson, C.M. (1989). "Improving Classroom Management: A School-Based Program for Beginning the Year." *Journal of Educational Research* 83, 2: 82–90.

Evertson, C.M., C.H. Anderson, L.M. Anderson, and J.E. Brophy. (1980). "Relationships Between Classroom Behaviors and Student Outcomes in Junior High Mathematics and English Classes." *American Educational Research Journal* 17, 1: 43–60.

Evertson, C.M., and E.T. Emmer. (1982). "Effective Management at the Beginning of the School Year in Junior High School Classes." *Journal of Educational Psychology* 74, 4: 485–498.

Evertson, C.M., and A.H. Harris. (1992). "What We Know About Managing Classrooms." *Educational Leadership* 49, 7: 74–78.

Floden, R., M. Buchmann, and J. Schwille. (1987). "Breaking with Everyday Experience." *Teachers College Record* 88, 4: 485–506.

Fraser, B.J. (1986). *Classroom Environment.* London: Groom Helm.

Gage, N.L. (1977). *The Scientific Basis of the Art of Teaching.* New York: Teachers College Press.

Gage, N.L. (November 1978). "The Yield of Research on Teaching." *Phi Delta Kappan* 60, 3: 229–235.

Gardner, H., and V. Boix-Mansilla. (1994). "Teaching for Understanding—Within and Across the Disciplines." *Educational Leadership* 51, 5: 14–18.

Good, T.L., and J.E. Brophy. (1984). *Looking in Classrooms,* 3rd ed. New York: Harper and Row.

Good, T.L., and J.E. Brophy. (1986). *Educational Psychology: A Realistic Approach,* 3rd ed. New York: Longman.

Goodwin, S.S., G.W. Sharp, E.F. Cloutier, and N.A. Diamond. (1983). "Effective Classroom Questioning." Paper identified by the Task Force on Establishing a National Clearinghouse of Materials Developed for Teaching Assistant (TA) Training. (ERIC Document Reproduction Service No. ED 285 497).

Goss, S.S., and G.M. Ingersoll. (1981). *Management of Disruptive and Off-Task Behaviors: Selected Resources.* Washington, D.C.: ERIC Clearinghouse on Teacher Education. (ERIC Document Reproduction Service No. SP 017 373).

Griffin, G. (1986). "Clinical Teacher Education." In *Reality and Reform in Clinical Teacher Education,* edited by J. Hoffman and S. Edwards. New York: Random House.

Grimmett, P., and G. Erickson, eds. (1988). *Reflection in Teacher Education.* New York: Teachers College Press.

Haertel, G., H.J. Walberg, and E. Haertel. (1981). "Sociopsychological

Environments and Learning." *British Educational Research Journal* 7: 27–36.

Heckman, P.E. (1994). "Planting Seeds: Understanding Through Investigation." *Educational Leadership* 51, 5: 36–39.

Hennes, M. (1921). "Project Teaching in an Advanced Fifth Grade." *Teachers College Record* 19, 2: 137–148.

Hilliard, A.G. (January 1989). "Teachers and Cultural Style in a Pluralistic Society." *NEA Today*, 65–69.

Hohn, R. (October 1986). "Research on Contextual Effects and Effective Teaching." Paper presented at the Midwestern Educational Research Association Conference, Chicago. (ERIC Document Reproduction Service No. ED 287 853).

Irvine, J.J. (1989). *Black Students and School Failure*. New York: Greenwood Press.

Irvine, J.J. (May 1990). "Beyond Role Models: The Influence of Black Teachers on Black Students." Paper presented at Educational Testing Service, Princeton, N.J.

Jones, J. (1992). *Praxis III Teacher Assessment Criteria Research Base*. Princeton, N.J.: Educational Testing Service.

Kauchak, D., and K. Peterson. (1987). *Teachers' Thoughts on the Assessment of Their Teaching*. Washington, D.C.: American Educational Research Association.

Keith, L., L.G. Tormatzky, and L.E. Pettigrew. (1974). "An Analysis of Verbal and Nonverbal Classroom Teaching Behaviors." *Journal of Experimental Education* 42, 4: 30–38.

Kemessis, S. (1987). "Critical Reflection." In *Staff Development for School Improvement,* edited by M. Wideen and I. Andrews. Philadelphia: Falmer Press.

Kilpatrick, W.H. (1918). "The Project Method." *Teachers College Record* 19, 4: 319–335.

Kilpatrick, W.H. (1925). *Foundations of Method: Informal Talks on Teaching*. New York: Macmillan.

Krupczak, W.P. (1972). "Relationships Among Student Self-Concept of Academic Ability, Teacher Perception of Student Academic Ability and Student Achievement." (Doctoral Diss., University of Miami). *Dissertation Abstracts International* 33, 3388A.

Leinhardt, G. (1992). "What Research on Learning Tells Us About Teaching." *Educational Leadership* 49, 7: 20–25.

Levin, H.M. (1987). "Accelerated Schools for Disadvantaged Students." *Educational Leadership* 44, 6: 19–21.

McCombs, B.L. (1992). *Learner-Centered Psychological Principles: Guidelines for School Redesign and Reform*. Washington, D.C.: American Psychological Association.

McCutcheon, G. (1980). "How Do Elementary School Teachers Plan? The Nature of Planning and Influences on It." In *Focus on Teaching*, edited by W. Doyle and T. Good. Chicago: University of Chicago Press.

Michaels, S. (1981). "Sharing Time: Children's Narrative Styles and Differential Access to Literacy." *Language in Society* 10: 423–442.

Moll, L.C. (1988). "Some Key Issues in Teaching Latino Students." *Language Arts* 65, 5: 465–472.

Moors, R. (1979). *Evaluating Educational Environments: Procedures, Methods, Findings and Policy Implications*. San Francisco: Jossey-Bass.

Morine-Dershimer, G. (1977). *What's in a Plan? Stated and Unstated Plans for Lessons*. Sacramento: California State Commission for Teacher Preparation and Licensing. (ERIC Document Reproduction Service No. ED 139 739).

National Board for Professional Teaching Standards. (1991). *Toward High and Rigorous Standards for the Teaching Profession*, 3rd ed. Detroit: Author.

Natriello, G. (1987). *Evaluation Processes in Schools and Classrooms*. (Report No. 12). Baltimore: Center for Social Organization of Schools. (ERIC Document Reproduction Service No. ED 294 890).

Newmann, F.M., W.G. Secada, and G.G. Wehlage. (1995). *A Guide to Authentic Instruction and Assessment: Vision, Standards, and Scoring*. Wisconsin Center for Education Research, Madison.

Nias, J., G. Southworth, and P. Campbell. (1992). *Whole School Curriculum Development in the Primary School.* London: The Falmer Press.

Oakes, J. (1986). "Tracking, Inequity, and the Rhetoric of School Reform: Why Schools Don't Change." *Journal of Education* 168, 1: 60–80.

Osborn, J.H., B.F. Jones, and M. Stein. (1985). "The Case for Improving Textbooks." *Educational Leadership* 42, 7: 9–16.

Pajares, M.F. (1992). "Teachers' Beliefs and Educational Research: Cleaning up a Messy Act." *Review of Educational Research* 62, 3: 307–332.

Perkins, D., and T. Blythe. (1994). "Putting Understanding up Front." *Educational Leadership* 51, 5: 4–7.

Perrone, V. (1994). "How to Engage Students in Learning." *Educational Leadership* 51, 5: 11–13.

Peterson, P.L., R.W. Marx, and C.M. Clark. (1978). "Teacher Planning, Teacher Behavior, and Student Achievement." *American Educational Research Journal* 15, 3: 417–432.

Porter, A.C., and J.E. Brophy. (June 1987). "Good Teaching: Insights from the Work of the Institute for Research on Teaching." (Occasional Paper No. 114). East Lansing: The Institute for Research on Teaching, Michigan State University.

Porter, A.C., and J.E. Brophy. (1988). "Synthesis of Research on Good Teaching: Insights from the Work of the Institute for Research on Teaching." *Educational Leadership* 45, 8: 74–85.

Powell, J.H., U. Casanova, and D.C. Berliner. (1991). *Parental Involvement: Readings in Educational Research, A Program for Professional Development, A National Education Association Project.* Washington, D.C.: National Education Association.

Reynolds, A. (1992). "What Is Competent Beginning Teaching? A Review of the Literature." *Review of Educational Research* 62, 1: 1–35.

Rist, R. (1970). "Student Social Class and Teacher Expectations: The Self-Fulfilling Prophecy in Ghetto Education." *Harvard Educational Review* 40, 3: 411–451.

Rosenfeld, M., N.E. Freeberg, and P. Bukatko. (1992). *The Professional Functions of Secondary School Teachers.* (Research Report 92–47). Princeton, N.J.: Educational Testing Service.

Rosenfeld, M., A. Reynolds, and P. Bukatko. (1992). *The Professional Functions of Elementary School Teachers.* (Research Report 92–53). Princeton, N.J.: Educational Testing Service.

Rosenfeld, M., G. Wilder, and P. Bukatko. (1992). *The Professional Functions of Middle School Teachers.* (Research Report 92–46). Princeton, N.J.: Educational Testing Service.

Rosenshine, B. (1971). *Teaching Behaviors and Student Achievement.* London: International Association for the Evaluation of Education.

Rosenshine, B. (1983). "Teaching Functions in Instructional Programs." *The Elementary School Journal* 83: 335–353.

Rosenshine, B. (1987). "Explicit Teaching." In *Talks to Teachers*, edited by D.C. Berliner and B.V. Rosenshine. New York: Random House.

Rosenshine, B., and N. Furst. (1971). "Research on Teacher Performance Criteria." In *Research in Teacher Education*, edited by B.O. Smith. Englewood Cliffs, N.J.: Prentice-Hall.

Rosenthal, R. (1973). "The Pygmalion Effect Lives." *Psychology Today* 7, 4: 56–60, 62–63.

Ross, J.A., and E.M. Regan. (1993). "Sharing Professional Experience: Its Impact on Professional Development." *Teaching and Teacher Education* 9, 1: 91–106.

Sanford. J.P., and C.M. Evertson. (1980). *Beginning the School Year at a Low SES Junior High: Three Case Studies.* Austin: The University of Texas at Austin, R&D Center for Teacher Education. (ERIC Document Reproduction Service No. ED 195 547).

Schön, D. (1987). *Educating the Reflective Practitioner: Toward a New Design for Teaching and Learning in the Professions.* San Francisco: Jossey-Bass.

Schunk, D.H. (1991). "Self-Efficacy and Academic Motivation." *Educational Psychologist* 26: 207–231.

Scriven, M. (1994). "Duties of the Teacher." *Journal of Personnel Evaluation in Education* 8, 2: 151–184.

Shulman, L.S. (1987). "Knowledge and Teaching: Foundations of the New Reform." *Harvard Educational Review* 57, 1: 1–22.

Sigel, I.E. (1990). "What Teachers Need to Know About Human Development." In *What Teachers Need to Know: The Knowledge, Skills, and Values Essential to Good Teaching*, D.D. Dill and Associates, San Francisco: Jossey-Bass.

Smith, L.R. (1985). "A Low-Inference Indicator of Lesson Organization." *Journal of Classroom Interaction* 21, 1: 25–30.

Smith, L.R., and K. Sanders. (1981). "The Effects of Student Achievement and Student Perception of Varying Structure in Social Studies Content." *Journal of Educational Research* 74, 5: 333–336.

Smylie, M.A. (1988). "The Enhancement Function of Staff Development: Organizational and Psychological Antecedents to Individual Teacher Change." *American Educational Research Journal* 25, 1: 1–30.

Stage, E. (1989). *Strategies and Materials for Meeting the Needs of All Students in Math, Science, Technology, and Health*. Sacramento: California Curriculum Commission.

Stallings, J.A. (1982). "Effective Strategies for Teaching Basic Skills." In *Developing Basic Skills Programs in Secondary Schools*, edited by D.G. Wallace. Alexandria, Va.: Association for Supervision and Curriculum Development.

Stallings, J.A., and D.H. Kaskowitz. (1974). *Follow-Through Classroom Evaluation, 1972–1993*. Menlo Park, Calif.: Stanford Research Institute (SRI) International.

Stein, M.K., and M.C. Wang. (1988). "Teacher Development and School Improvement: The Process of Teacher Change." *Teaching and Teacher Education* 4, 2: 171–187.

"Strategies for Success." (November 1994). *Educational Leadership* 52, 3: entire issue.

Sykes, G., and T. Bird. (August 1992). "Teacher Education and the Case Idea." *Review of Research in Education* 18: 457–521.

Tabachnick, B.R., and K. Zeichner, K. (1991). "Reflections on Reflective Teaching." In *Issues and Practices in Inquiry-Oriented Teacher Education*, edited by B. Tabachnick and K. Zeichner.

Philadelphia: Falmer Press.

Taylor, A., and B. Valentine. (1985). *Effective Schools. What Research Says About . . . Series, No. 1, Data-Search Reports*. Washington, D.C.: National Education Association. (ERIC Document Reproduction Service No. ED 274 073).

U. S. Department of Education. (1987). *What Works: Research About Teaching and Learning*. Washington, D.C.: U.S. Government Printing Office.

Van Patten, J., C. Chao, and C. Reigeluth. (1986). "A Review of Strategies for Sequencing and Synthesizing Instruction." *Review of Educational Research* 56, 4: 437–471.

Villegas, A.M. (1991). "Culturally Responsive Pedagogy for the 1990s and Beyond." Unpublished manuscript. Princeton, N.J.: Educational Testing Service.

Walberg, H., D. Schiller, and G.D. Haertel. (1979). "The Great Revolution in Educational Research." *Phi Delta Kappan* 61, 3: 179–182.

Walker, H. (1985). *Teacher Social Behavior Standards and Expectations as Determinants of Classroom Ecology, Teacher Behavior, and Child Outcomes: Final Report*. Eugene: Center for Educational Policy and Management, University of Oregon.

Weiss, J., and W. Louden. (1989). "Clarifying the Notion of Reflection." Paper presented at the annual meeting of the American Educational Research Association, San Francisco.

Williams, P.S. (1988). "Going West to Get East: Using Metaphors as Instructional Tools." *Journal of Children in Contemporary Society* 20, 1–2: 79–98.

Wiske, M.S. (1994). "How Teaching for Understanding Changes the Rules in the Classroom." *Educational Leadership* 51, 5: 19–21.

Wittrock, M.C., ed. (1986). *Handbook of Research on Teaching*, 3rd ed. New York: Macmillan.

Wolf, D.P. (1987). "The Art of Questioning." *Academic Connections*. New York: The College Board.

Wolk, S. (1994). "Project-Based Learning: Pursuits with a Purpose." *Educational Leadership* 52, 3: 42–45.

Woods, R.K. (1994). "A Close-Up Look at How Children Learn Science." *Educational Leadership* 51, 5: 33–35.

Yinger, R. (1977). *A Study of Teacher Planning: Description and Theory Development Using Ethnographic and Information Processing Methods.* Unpublished doctoral diss., Michigan State University, East Lansing.

Ysseldyke, J., S. Christenson, and M.L. Thurlow. (1987). *Instructional Factors That Influence Student Achievement: An Integrative Review.* (Monograph No. 7). Minneapolis: University of Minnesota Instructional Alternatives Project.

Zigmond, N., J. Sansone, S. Miller, K. Donahoe, and R. Kohnke. (1986). "Teaching Learning Disabled Students at the Secondary School Level: What Research Says to Teachers." *Learning Disabilities Focus* 1, 2: 108–115.

BIBLIOGRAPHY

Anderson, A.B. (1991). "Teaching Children: What Teachers Should Know." In *Teaching Academic Subjects to Diverse Learners*, edited by M.M. Kennedy. New York: Teachers College Press.

Arreaga-Mayer, C., and C. Greenwood. (1986). "Environmental Variables Affecting the School Achievement of Culturally and Linguistically Different Learners: An Instructional Perspective." *NABE: Journal for the National Association of Bilingual Education* 10, 2: 113–35.

Ashton, P.T., and R.B. Webb. (1986). *Making a Difference: Teachers' Sense of Efficacy and Student Achievement*. New York: Longman.

Austria, R.H. (1993). *Praxis III: Classroom Performance Assessments, The Delaware Collaboration, March 1991–August 1992*. Princeton, N.J.: Educational Testing Service.

Ayers, W. (1993). *To Teach: The Journey of a Teacher*. New York: Teachers College Press.

Brophy, J.E., and J.G. Putnam. (1979). *Classroom Management in the Elementary Grades: A Literature Review*. East Lansing: Institute for Research on Teaching, Michigan State University.

Cazden, C., and H. Mehan. (1989). "Principles from Sociology and Anthropology: Context, Code, Classroom, and Culture." In

Knowledge Base for the Beginning Teacher, edited by M.C. Reynolds. New York: Pergamon.

Clark, C.M. (1993). "What Makes a Good Teacher?" *Doubts and Certainties: A Forum on School Transformation from the NEA National Center for Innovation* 7, 4: 1–5.

Clark, C.M., and P.L. Peterson. (1986). "Teachers' Thought Processes." In *Handbook of Research on Teaching*, 3rd ed., edited by M.C. Wittrock. New York: Macmillan.

Cohen, D.K., M.W. McLaughlin, and J.E. Talbert. (1993). *Teaching for Understanding: Challenges for Policy and Practice.* San Francisco: Jossey-Bass.

Cooper, H., and T.L. Good. (1983). *Pygmalion Grows Up: Studies in the Expectation Communication Process.* New York: Longman.

Corno, L., and R.E. Snow. (1986). "Adapting Teaching to Individual Differences Among Learners." In *Handbook of Research on Teaching,* 3rd ed., edited by M.C. Wittrock. New York: Macmillan.

Darling-Hammond, L. (1989). "Accountability for Professional Practice." *Teachers College Record* 91, 1: 59–80.

Delpit, L.D. (1988). "The Silenced Dialogue: Power and Pedagogy in Educating Other People's Children." *Harvard Educational Review* 58, 3: 280–298.

Diaz, S., L.C. Moll, and H. Mehan. (1986). "Sociocultural Resources in Instruction: A Context-Specific Approach." In *Beyond Language: Social and Cultural Factors in Schooling Language Minority Students,* California State Department of Education. Los Angeles: California State University Evaluation, Dissemination, and Assessment Center.

Dill, D.D., and Associates. (1990). *What Teachers Need to Know: The Knowledge, Skills, and Values Essential to Good Teaching.* San Francisco: Jossey-Bass.

Dunkin, M., and B. Biddle. (1974). *The Study of Teaching.* New York: Holt, Rinehart and Winston.

Dwyer, C.A. (1991). "Measurement and Research Issues in Teacher Assessment." *Educational Psychologist* 26, 1: 3–22.

Dwyer, C.A. (1993). "Teaching and Diversity: Meeting the Challenges for Innovative Teacher Assessments." *Journal of Teacher Education* 44, 2: 119–129.

Emmer, E.T., and A. Aussiker. (1990). "School and Classroom Discipline Programs: How Well Do They Work?" In *Student Discipline Strategies,* edited by O.C. Moles. Albany: State University of New York Press.

Englemann, S. (1991). "Teachers, Schemata, and Instruction." In *Teaching Academic Subjects to Diverse Learners,* edited by M.M. Kennedy. New York: Teachers College Press.

Evertson, C.M. (1985). "Training Teachers in Classroom Management: An Experimental Study in Secondary School Classrooms." *Journal of Educational Research* 79, 1: 51–57.

Evertson, C.M., E.T. Emmer, J.P. Sanford, and B.S. Clements. (1983). "Improving Classroom Management: An Experiment in Elementary School Classrooms." *Elementary School Journal* 84, 173–188.

Evertson, C.M., E.T. Emmer, J.P. Sanford, B.S. Clements, and J. Martin. (March 1983). "Improving Junior High Classroom Management." Paper presented at the annual meeting of the American Educational Research Association, Montreal.

Floden, R.E. (1991). "What Teachers Need to Know About Learning." In *Teaching Academic Subjects to Diverse Learners,* edited by M.M. Kennedy. New York: Teachers College Press.

Fogarty, J., M. Wang, and R. Creek. (1983). "A Descriptive Study of Experienced and Novice Teachers' Interactive Instructional Thoughts and Actions." *Journal of Educational Research* 77, 1: 22–32.

Gage, N.L. (1974). "Evaluating Ways to Help Teachers to Behave Desirably." In *Competency Assessment Research and Evaluation: A Report of a National Conference, March 12–15, 1974.* Houston: University of Houston.

Gallimore, R. (May 1985). "The Accommodation of Instruction to Cultural Differences." Paper presented at the University of California Conference on the Underachievement of Linguistic Minorities, Lake Tahoe, Calif.

Gardner, H. (1992). *The Unschooled Mind: How Children Think and How Schools Should Teach.* New York: Basic Books.

Gettinger, M. (1986). "Issues and Trends in Academic-Engaged Time of Students." *Special Services in the Schools* 2, 4: 1–17.

Glaser, R. (1984). "Education and Thinking: The Role of Knowledge." *American Psychologist* 39, 2: 91–104.

Glasser, W. (1975). *Schools Without Failure.* New York: Harper and Row.

Good, T.L. (1990). "Building the Knowledge Base of Teaching." In *What Teachers Need to Know: The Knowledge, Skills, and Values Essential to Good Teaching*, D.D. Dill and Associates. San Francisco: Jossey-Bass.

Good, T.L., and D. Grouws. (1975). *Process-Product Relationships in 4th Grade Mathematics Classes.* Columbia: University of Missouri College of Education.

Grant, C.A. (1991). "Culture and Teaching: What Do Teachers Need to Know?" In *Teaching Academic Subjects to Diverse Learners*, edited by M.M. Kennedy. New York: Teachers College Press.

Heath, S.B. (1983). "Questioning at Home and in School: A Comparative Study." In *Doing Ethnography: Educational Anthropology in Action*, edited by G. Spindler. New York: Holt, Rinehart, and Winston.

Heath, S.B. (1983). *Ways with Words: Language, Life and Work in Communities and Classrooms.* London: Cambridge University Press.

Herman, S.H., and J. Tramontana. (1971). "Instructions and Group Versus Individual Reinforcement in Modifying Disruptive Group Behavior." *Journal of Applied Behavior Analysis* 4, 2: 113–119.

Holliday, B.G. (1985). "Differential Effects of Children's Self-Perceptions and Teachers' Perceptions on Black Children's Academic Achievement." *Journal of Negro Education* 54: 71–81.

Hollins, E. (1989). *A Conceptual Framework for Selecting Instructional Approaches and Materials for Inner-City Black Youngsters.* Sacramento: California Curriculum Commission.

Kagan, D.M. (1990). "Ways of Evaluating Teacher Cognition: Inferences Concerning the Goldilocks Principle." *Review of Educational Research* 60, 3: 419–469.

Karweit, N. (1988). "Time-On-Task: The Second Time Around." *NASSP Bulletin* 72, 505: 31–39.

Katz, L.G., and J.D. Raths. (1985). "A Framework for Research on Teacher Education Programs." *Journal of Teacher Education* 36, 6: 9–15.

Klem, L. (April 1990). "The Challenge of Understanding State Content Area Requirements for the Licensing of Teachers." In *Defining the Job of the Beginning Teacher: Multiple Views.* C. Dwyer (chair), Symposium conducted at the annual meeting of the American Educational Research Association, Boston.

Klem, L. (1992). *STAT State Information Tables, 1992.* Princeton, N.J.: Educational Testing Service.

Klem, L. (1993a). *CHART.* Princeton, N.J.: Educational Testing Service.

Klem, L. (1993b). *STAT.* Princeton, N.J.: Educational Testing Service.

Klem, L. (1993c). *Project MATCH.* Princeton, N.J.: Educational Testing Service.

Kochman, T. (1981). *Black and White Styles in Conflict.* Chicago: University of Chicago Press.

Kuligowski, B., D. Holdzkom, and R.L. French. (1993). "Teacher Performance Evaluation in the Southeastern States: Forms and Functions." *Journal of Personnel Evaluation in Education* 6, 4: 335–358.

Little, J.W. (1992). *Teachers' Professional Development in a Climate of Educational Reform.* Berkeley, Calif.: Consortium on Policy Research in Education.

Livingston, S. (1993). *Inter-Assessor Consistency of the Praxis III: Classroom Performance Assessments: Spring 1992 Preliminary Version.* Princeton, N.J.: Educational Testing Service.

Logan, C.S., J.S. Garland, and C.D. Ellett. (1989). "Large-Scale Teacher Performance Assessment Instruments: A Synthesis of What They Measure and a National Survey of Their Influence on the Preparation of Teachers." Paper presented at the annual meeting of the American Educational Research Association, San Francisco, Calif.

Marzano, R.J., R.S. Brandt, C.S. Hughes, B.F. Jones, B.Z. Presseisen, S.C. Rankin, and C. Suhor. (1988). *Dimension of Thinking: A Framework for Curriculum and Instruction*. Alexandria, Va.: Association for Supervision and Curriculum Development.

McDiarmid, G.W. (1991). "What Teachers Need to Know About Cultural Diversity: Restoring Subject Matter to the Picture." In *Teaching Academic Subjects to Diverse Learners,* edited by M.M. Kennedy. New York: Teachers College Press.

McDonald, F.J. (Spring 1976). "Report on Phase II of the Beginning Teacher Evaluation Study." *Journal of Teacher Education* 27, 1: 39–42.

Merwin, J.C. (1989). "Evaluation." In *Knowledge Base for the Beginning Teacher*, edited by M.C. Reynolds. New York: Pergamon.

Messick, S. (1992). "Validity." In *Educational Measurement*, 3rd ed., edited by R.L. Linn. New York: Macmillan.

Myford, C., A.M. Villegas, A. Reynolds, R. Camp, J. Jones, J. Knapp, E. Mandinach, L. Morris, and B. Sjostrom. (1993). *Formative Studies of Praxis III: Classroom Performance Assessments, an Overview*. Princeton, N.J.: Educational Testing Service.

Nelson-Barber, S., and T. Meier. (1990). "Multicultural Context a Key Factor in Teaching." *Academic Connections*. New York: The College Board.

Paine, L. (1989). "Orientation Towards Diversity: What Do Prospective Teachers Bring?" (Research Report 89-9). East Lansing, Mich.: National Center for Research on Teacher Education.

Pinnegar, S. (1989). *Teachers' Knowledge of Students and Classrooms*. Unpublished doctoral diss., University of Arizona, Tucson.

Powers, D.E. (1992). *Assessing the Classroom Performance of Beginning Teachers: Educators' Appraisal of Proposed Evaluation Criteria*. (Research Report 92-56). Princeton, N.J.: Educational Testing Service.

Rodriguez, Y.E.G., B.R. Sjostrom, and A.M. Villegas. (1993). "Approaches to Cultural Diversity in the Classroom: Implications for Teacher Education." Paper presented at the annual meeting of the American Association of Colleges for Teacher Education, San Diego.

Rosenshine, B., and R. Stevens. (1986). "Teaching Functions." In *Handbook of Research on Teaching*, 3rd ed., edited by M.C. Wittrock. New York: Macmillan.

Rutter, M., B. Maugham, P. Mortimore, J. Ouston, and A. Smith. (1979). *Fifteen Thousand Hours: Secondary Schools and Their Effects on Children*. Cambridge, Mass.: Harvard University Press.

Shulman, L.S. (1988a). "A Union of Insufficiencies: Strategies for Teacher Assessment in a Period of Educational Reform." *Educational Leadership* 46, 3: 36–41.

Shulman, L.S. (1988b). "The Paradox of Teacher Assessment." In *New Directions for Teacher Assessment: Proceedings of the 1988 ETS Invitational Conference*. Princeton, N.J.: Educational Testing Service.

Shulman, J. (1989). "Blue Freeways: Traveling the Alternate Route with Big City Teacher Trainees." *Journal of Teacher Education* 40, 2–8.

Simmons, R. (1994). "The Horse Before the Cart: Assessing for Understanding." *Educational Leadership* 51, 5: 22–23.

Sparks-Langer, G.M., J.M. Simmons, M. Pasch, A.B. Colton, and A. Starko. (1990). "Reflective Pedagogical Thinking: How Can We Promote It and Measure It?" *Journal of Teacher Education* 41, 4: 23–32.

Stepien, W., and S. Gallagher. (1993). "Problem-Based Learning: As Authentic as It Gets." *Educational Leadership* 50, 7: 25–28.

Stepien, W., S. Gallagher, and D. Workman. (1993). "Problem-Based Learning for Traditional and Interdisciplinary Classrooms." *Journal for the Education of the Gifted* 16, 4: 338–357.

Sternberg, R.J., and R.K. Wagner. (1993). "The G-Centric View of Intelligence and Job Performance Is Wrong." *Current Directions in Psychological Science* 2, 1: 1–4.

Stodolsky, S.S. (1988). *The Subject Matters*. Chicago: University of Chicago Press.

Street, M.S. (1991). *Content Synthesis of Currently Used Statewide Performance Assessment Instruments*. Princeton, N.J.: Educational Testing Service.

Tracy, S.J., and P. Smeaton. (1992). "State-Mandated Assisting and Assessing Teachers: Levels of State Control." *Journal of Personnel Evaluation in Education* 6, 3: 219–234.

Unger, C. (1994) "What Teaching for Understanding Looks Like." *Educational Leadership* 51, 5: 8–10.

Villegas, A.M. (1992). "The Competence Needed by Beginning Teachers in a Multicultural Society." Paper presented at the annual meeting of the American Association of Colleges of Teacher Education, San Antonio, Tex..

Vosniadou, S. (1992). "Knowledge Acquisition and Conceptual Change." *Applied Psychology: An International Review* 41: 347–357.

Wesley, S., M. Rosenfeld, and A. Sims-Gunzenhauser. (1993). *Assessing the Classroom Performance of Beginning Teachers: Teachers' Judgments of Evaluation Criteria*. Princeton, N.J.: Educational Testing Service.

Wilkins, R.G. (1993). *Praxis III: Classroom Performance Assessments, Collaborative Fieldwork in Minnesota, March 1991–October 1992*. Princeton, N.J.: Educational Testing Service.

Wong-Fillmore, L.W. (1990). *Now or Later? Issues Related to the Early Education of Minority Group Students*. Washington, D.C.: Council of Chief State School Officers.

Woolfolk, A.E., and W.K. Hoy. (1990). "Prospective Teachers' Sense of Efficacy and Beliefs About Control." *Journal of Educational Psychology* 82, 1: 81–91.

Zahorik, J.A. (1975). "Teachers' Planning Models." *Educational Leadership* 33, 2: 134–139.